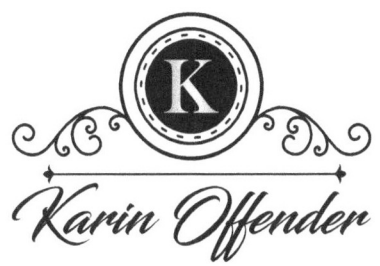

Karin Offender

Coloring Test Pages

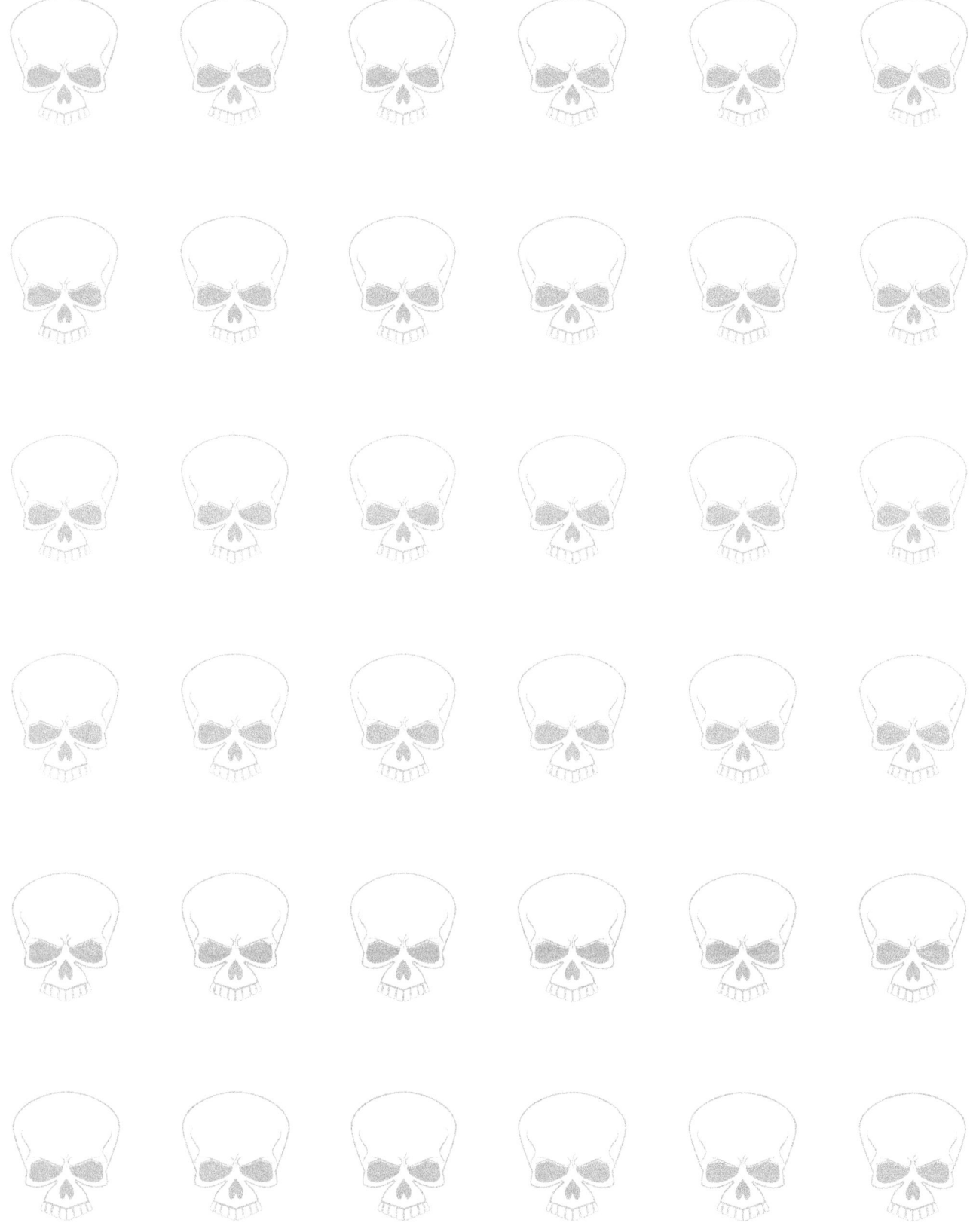

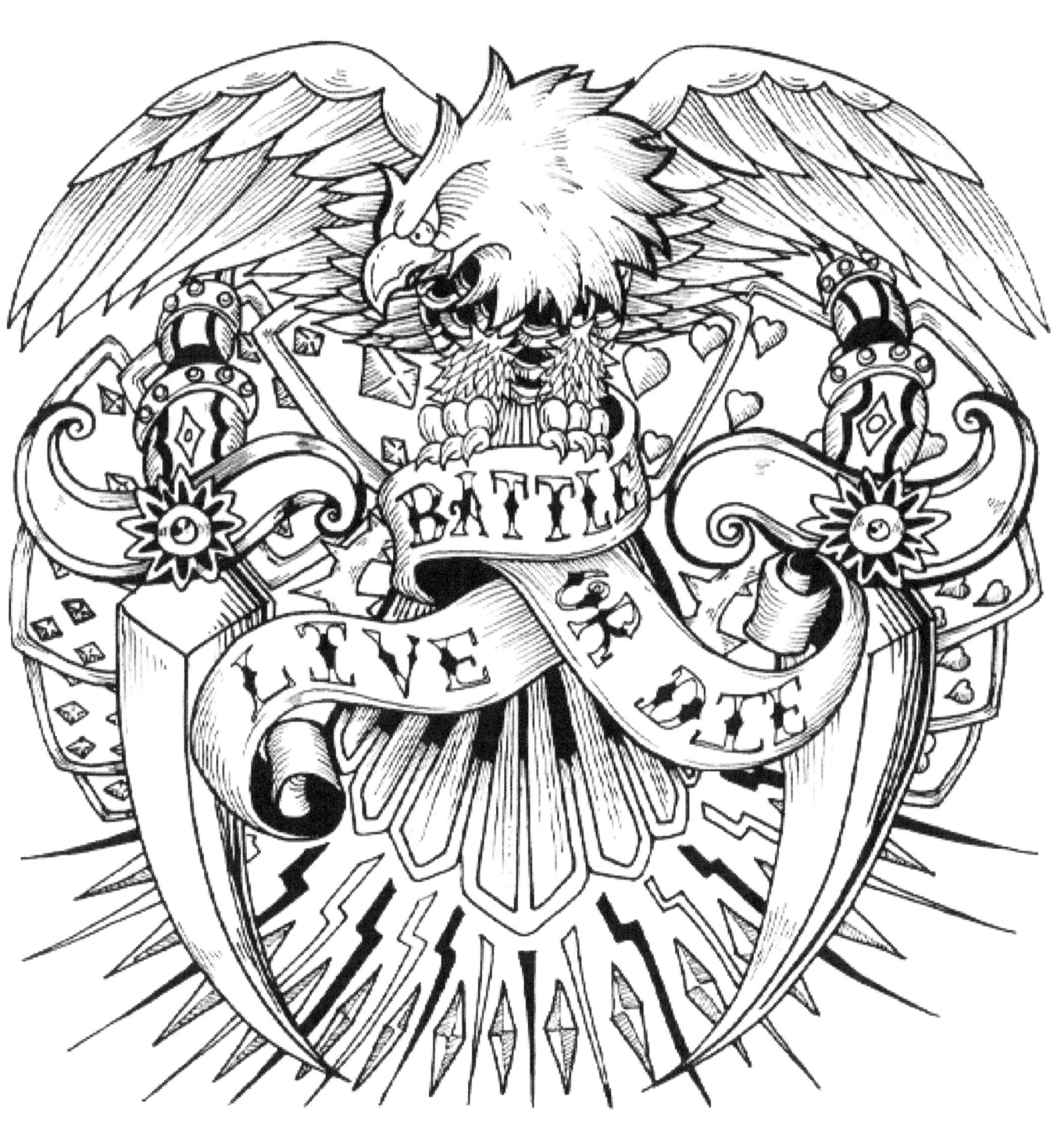

Coloring Test Pages

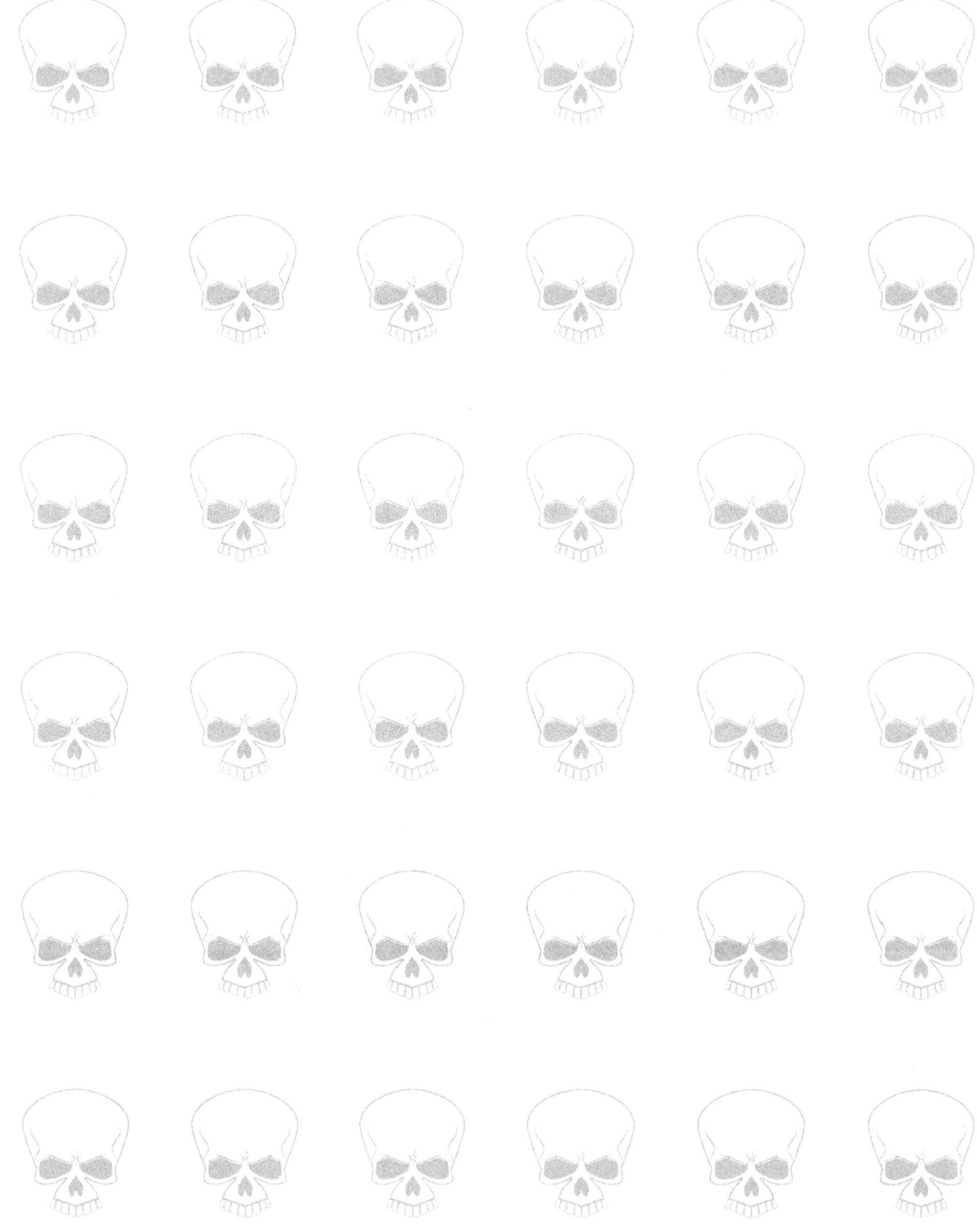

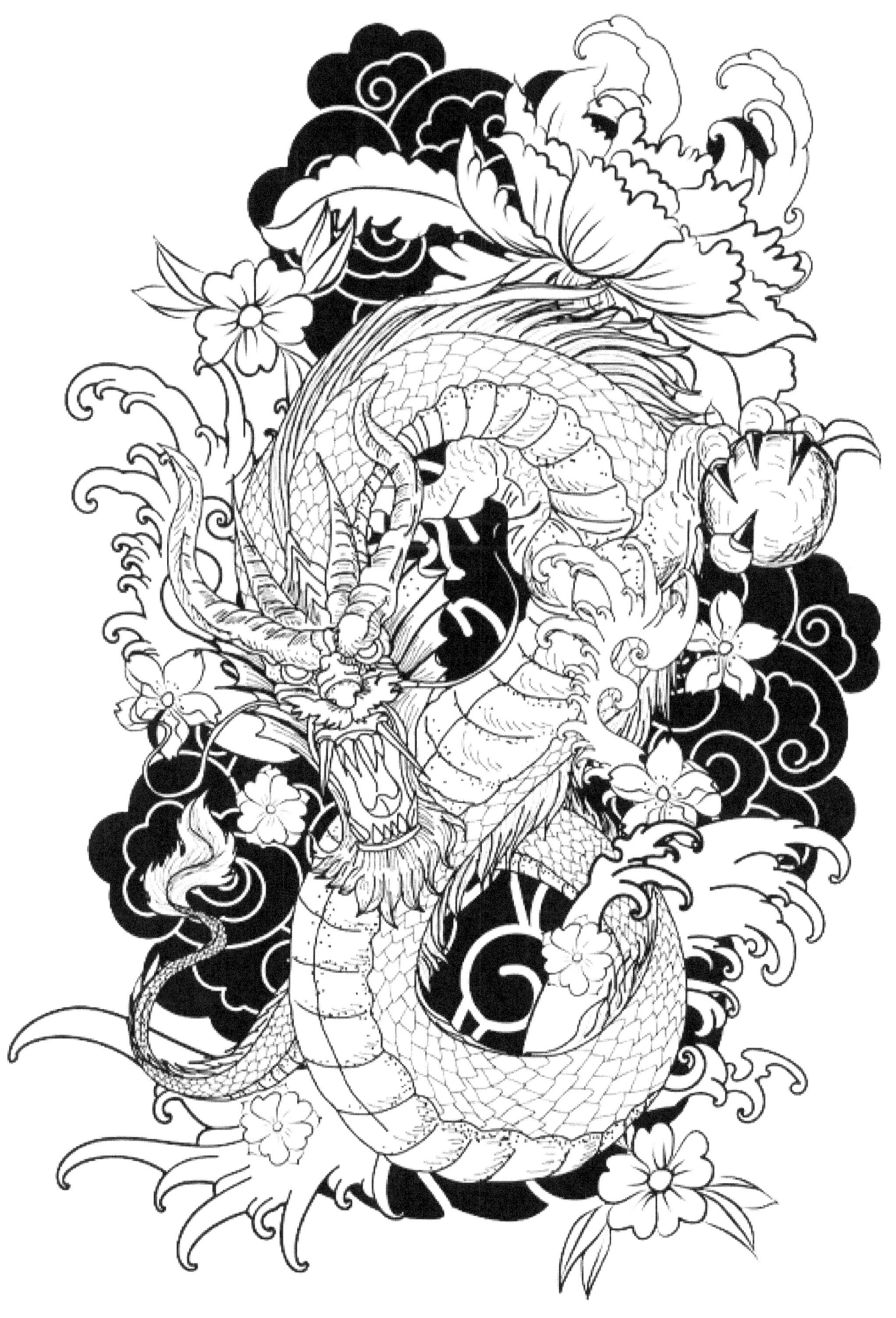

Coloring Test Pages

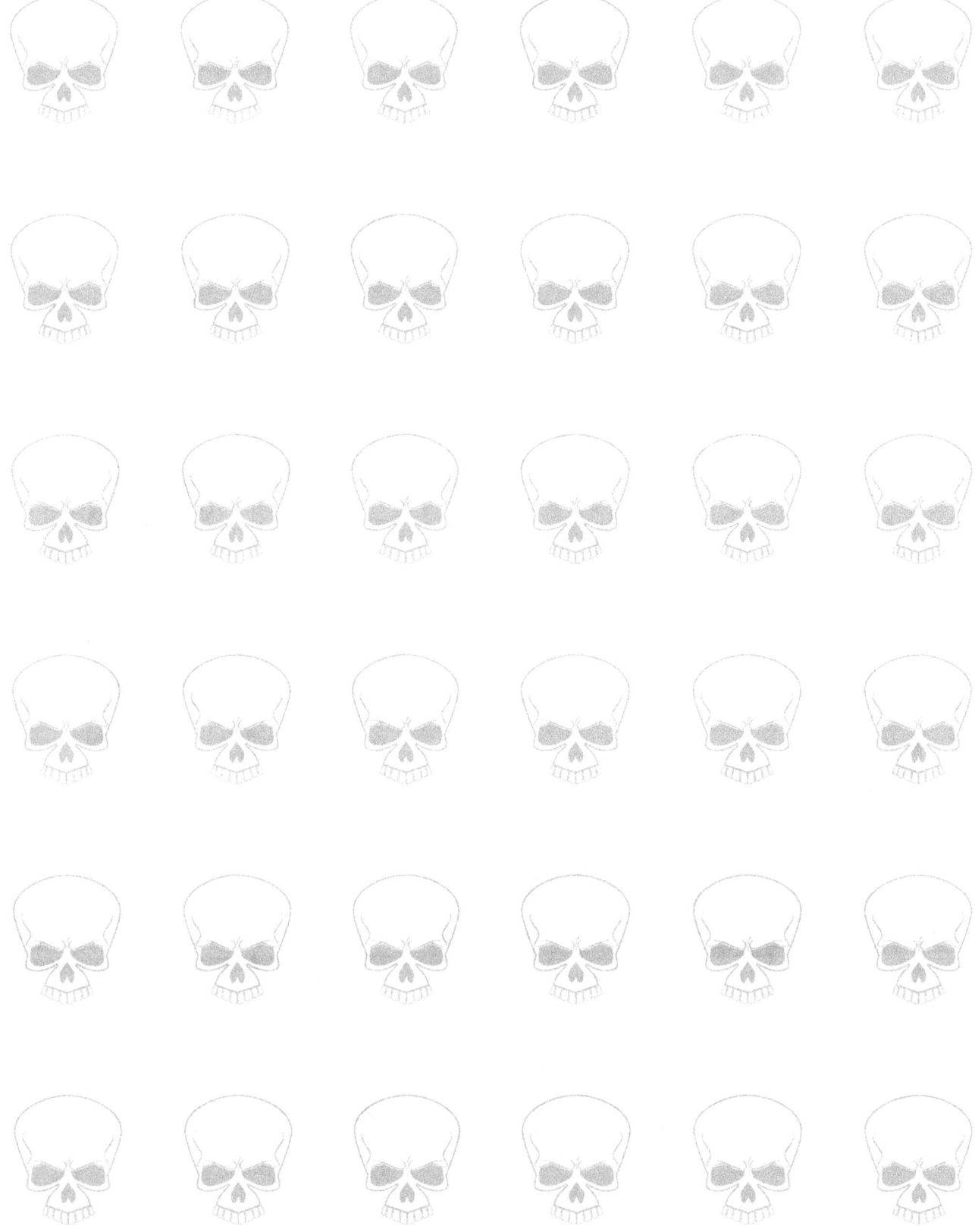

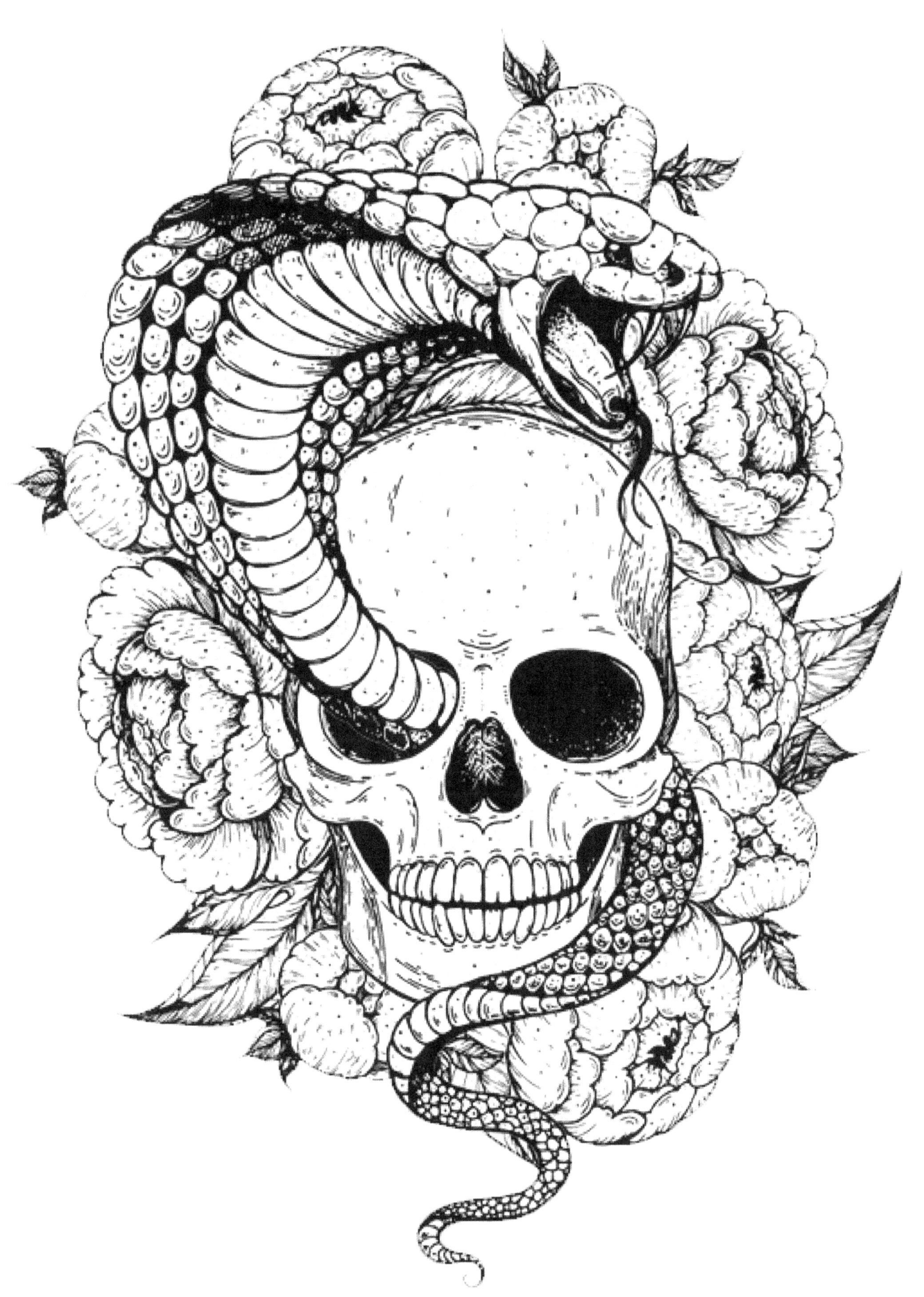

Coloring Test Pages

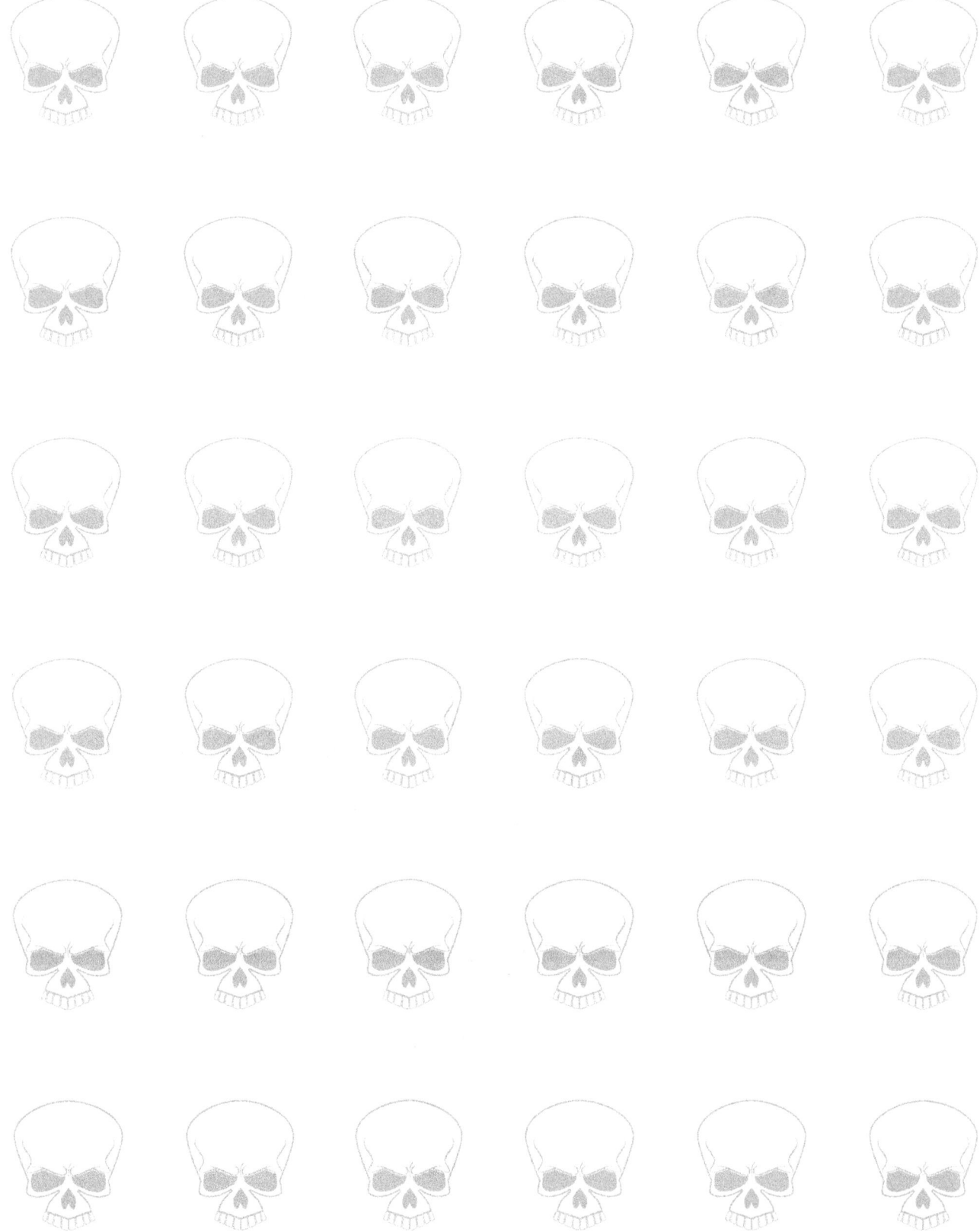

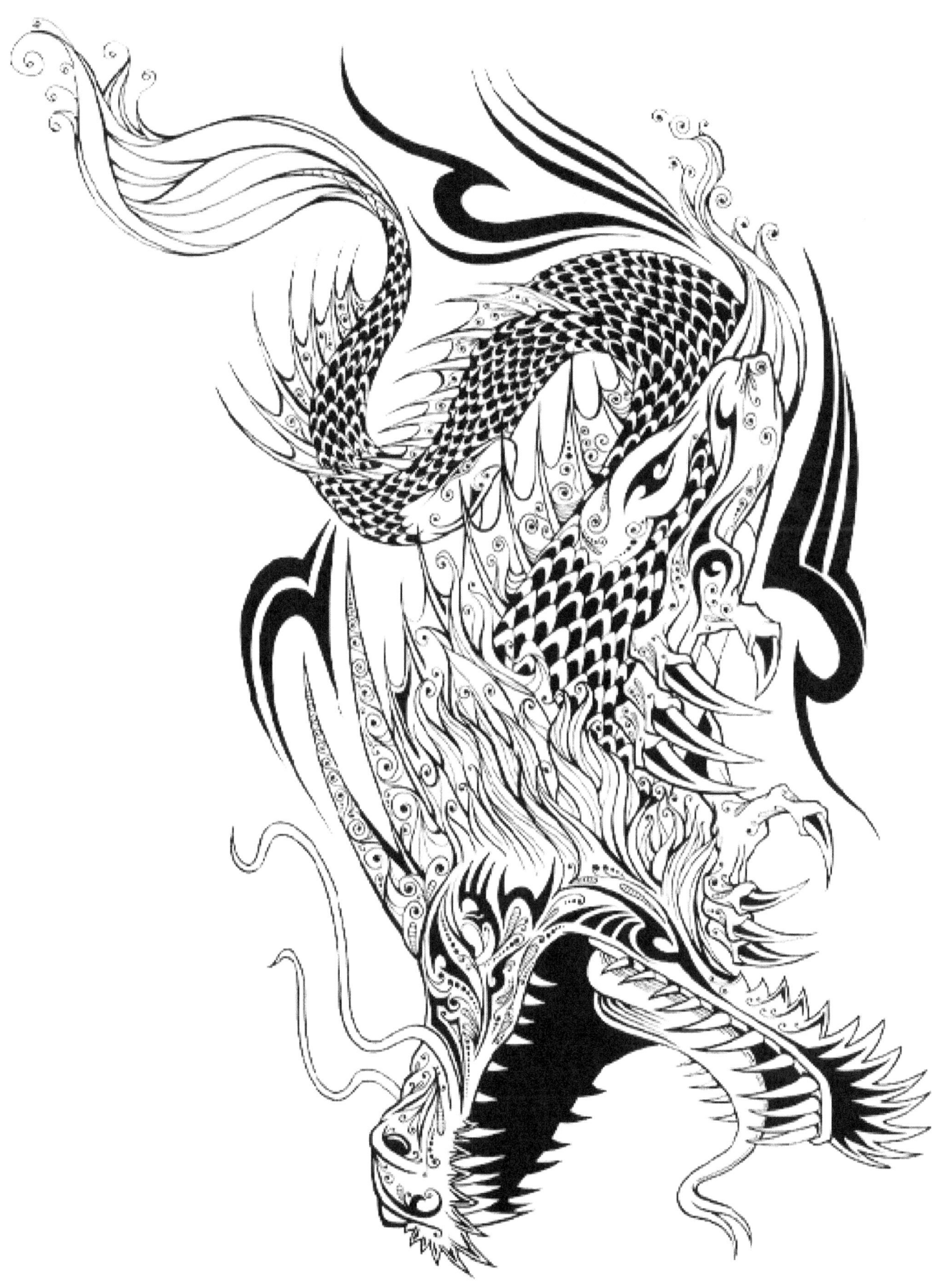

Coloring Test Pages

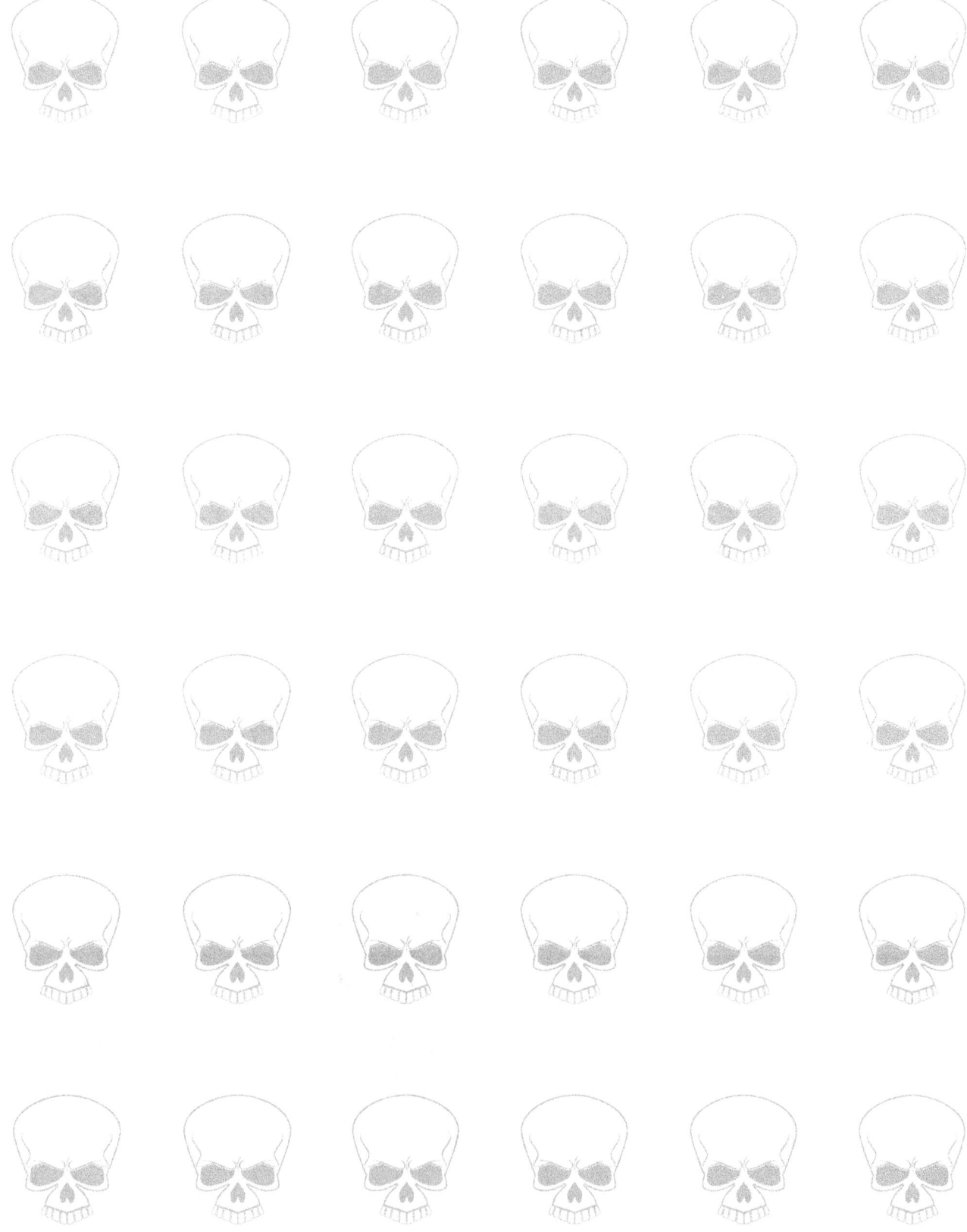

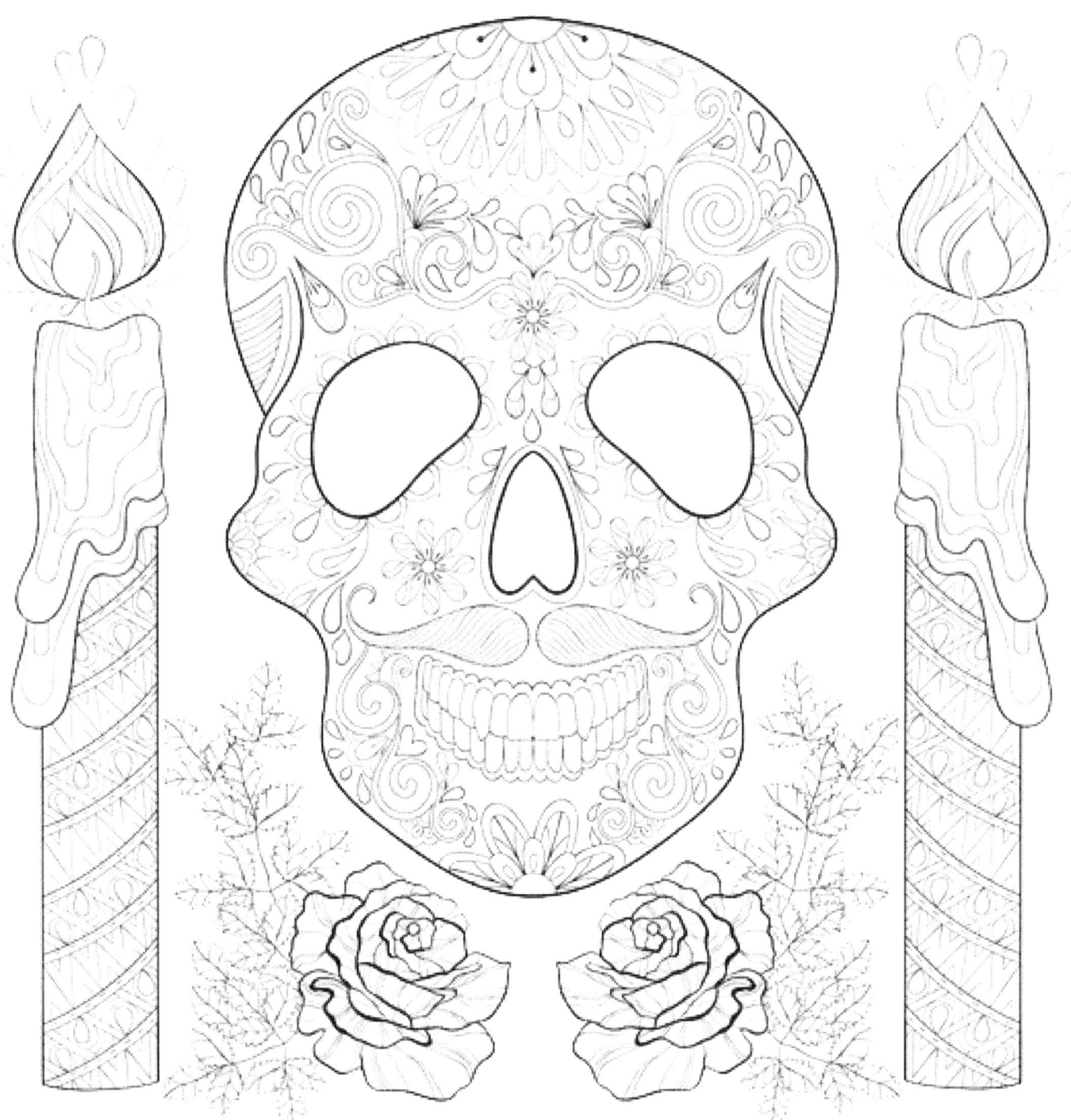

Coloring Test Pages

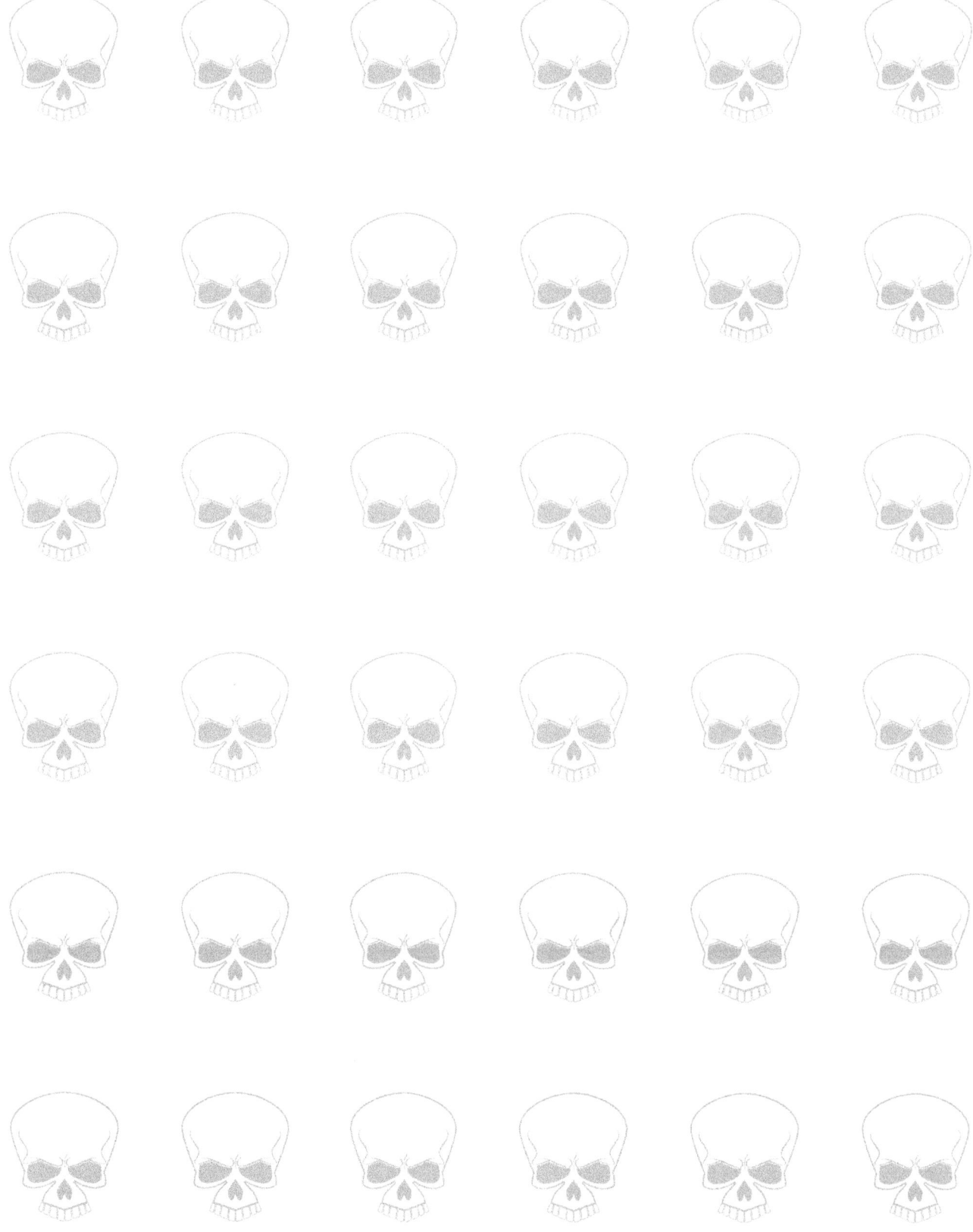

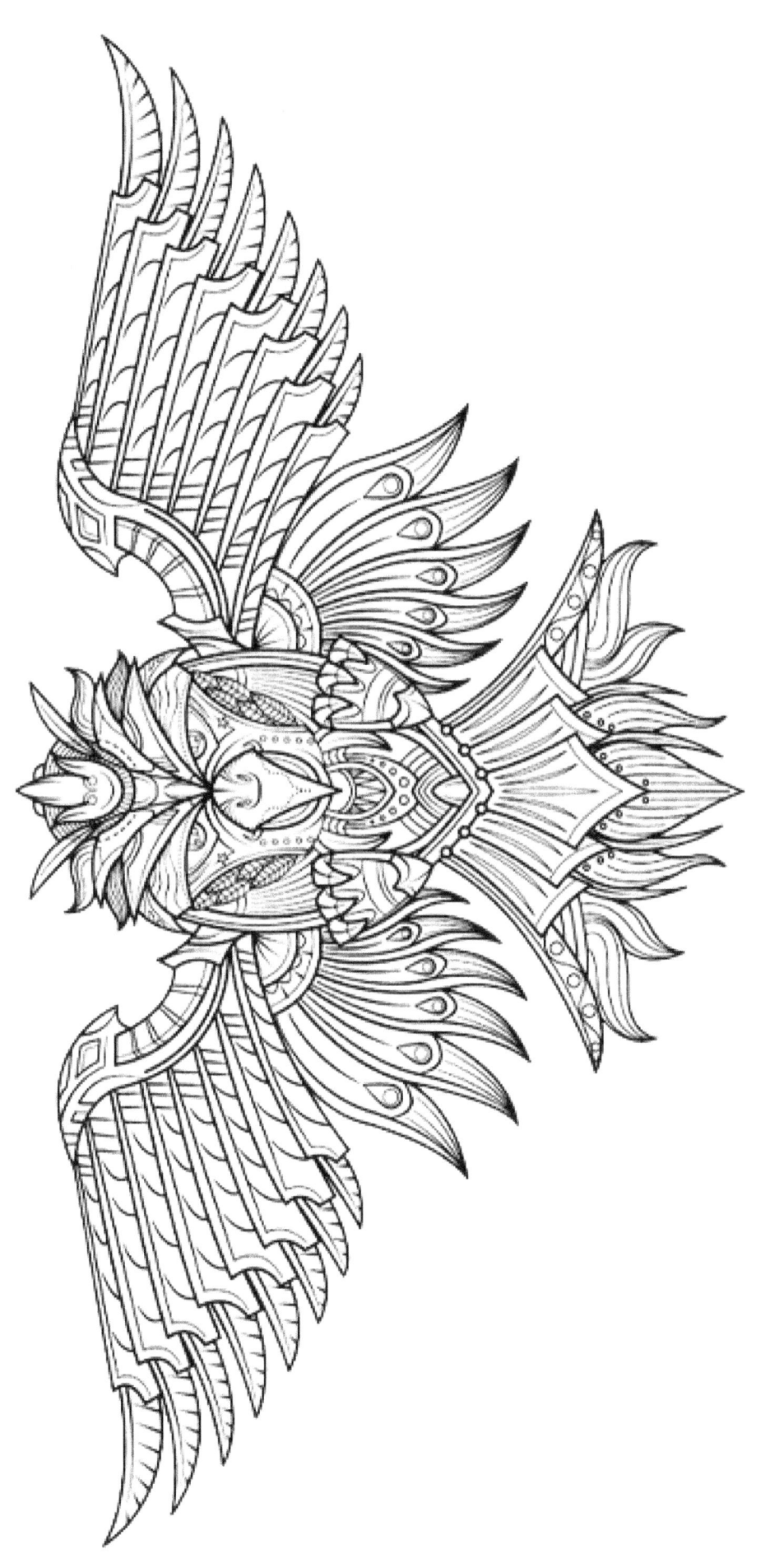

Coloring Test Pages

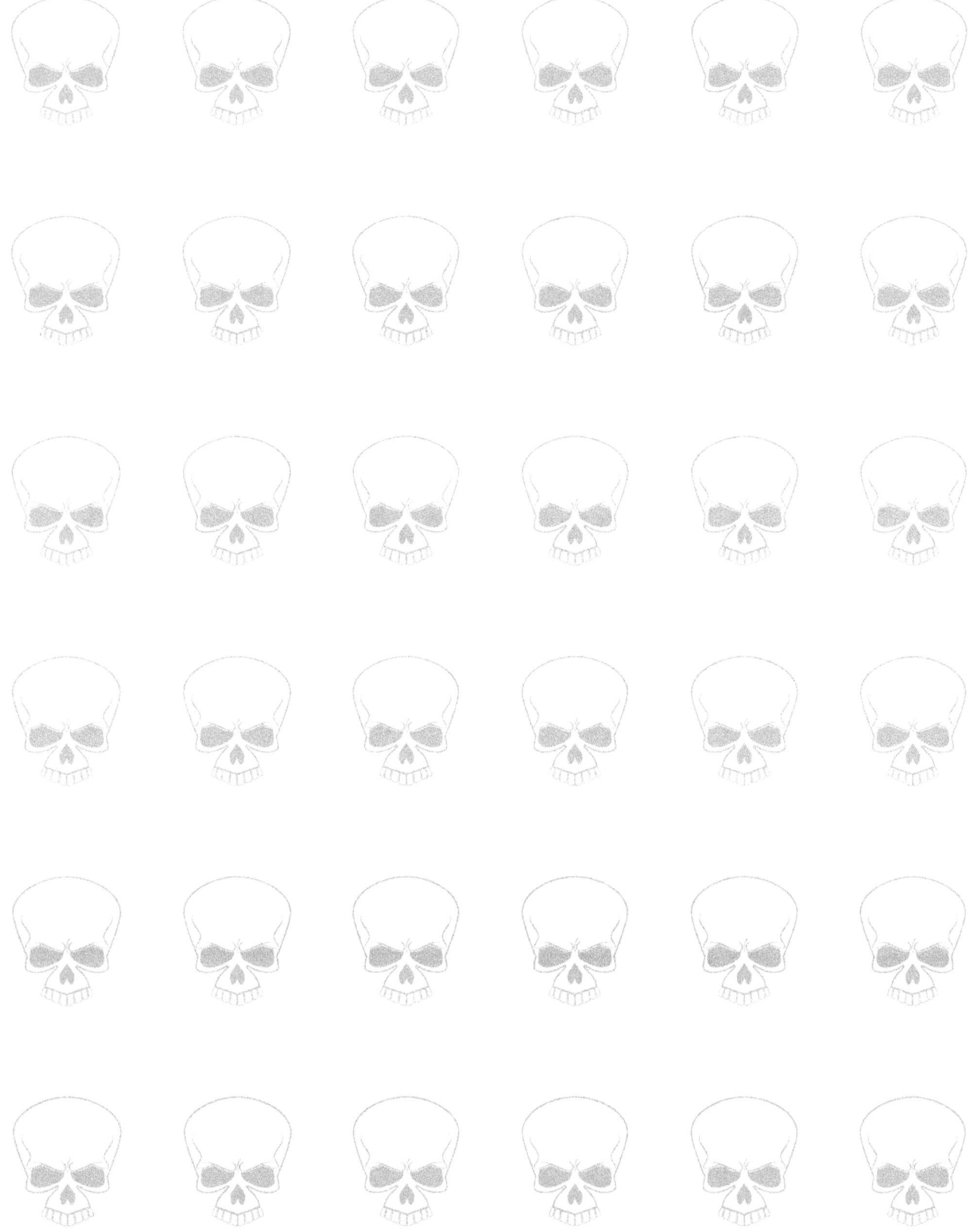

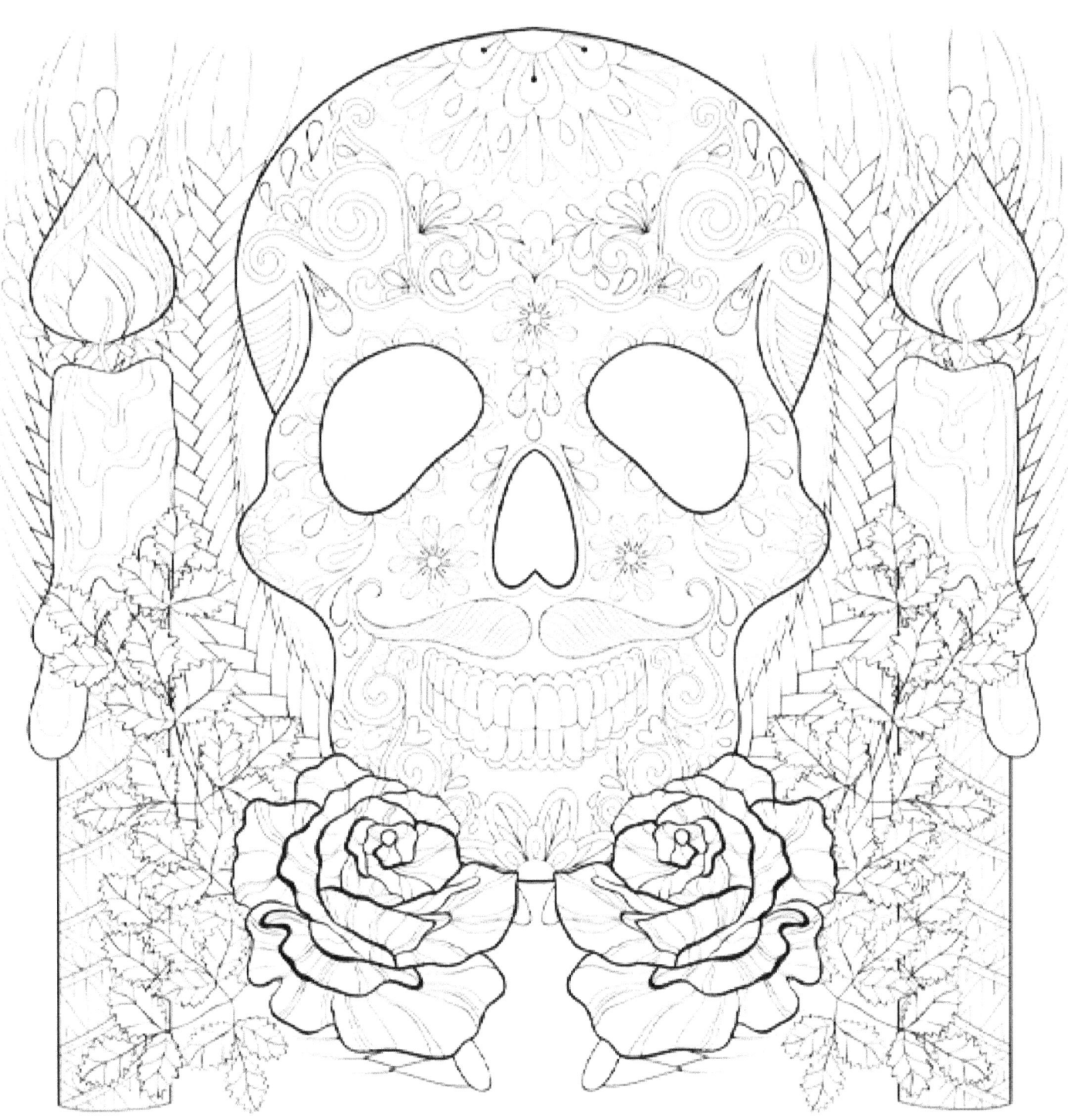

Coloring Test Pages

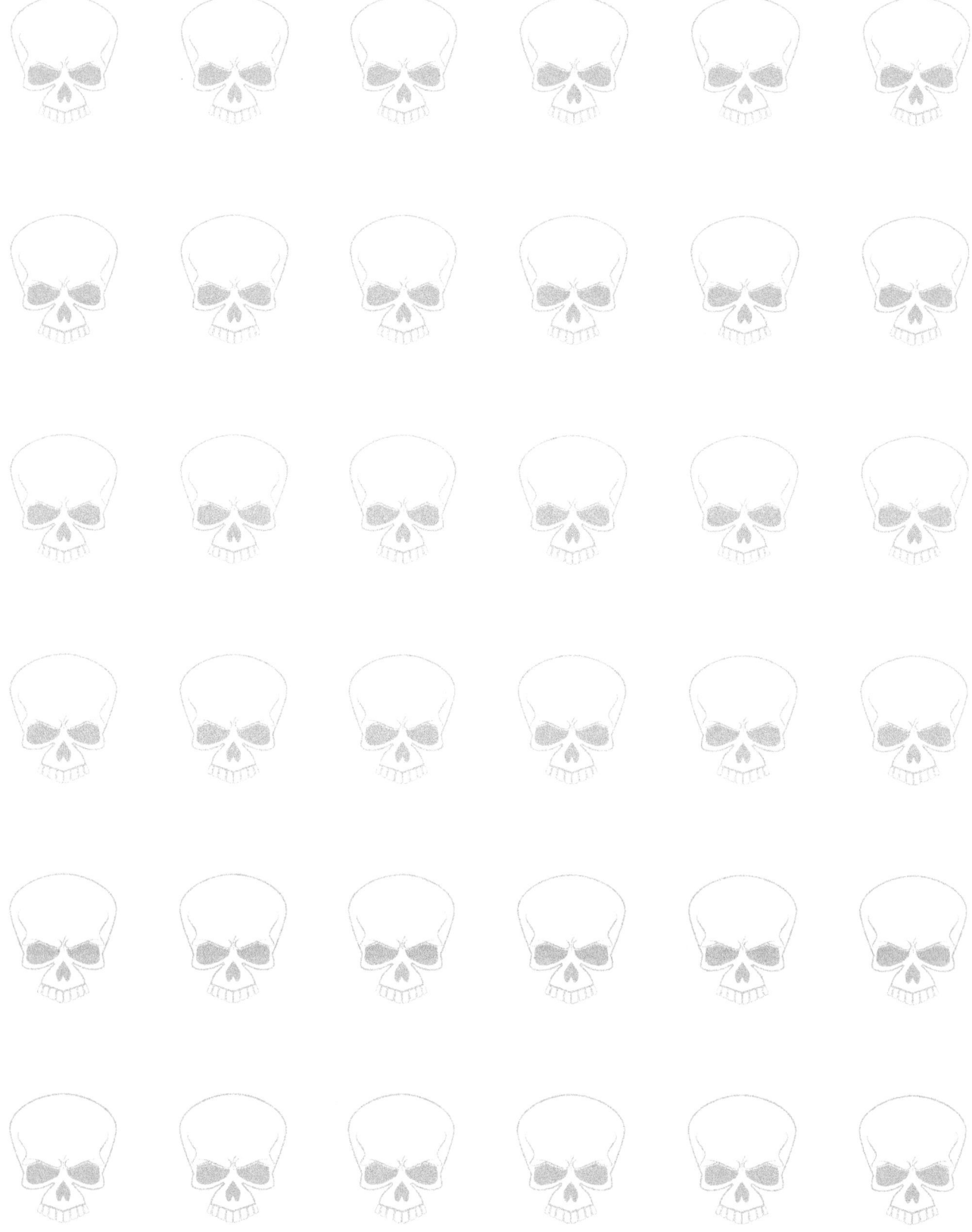

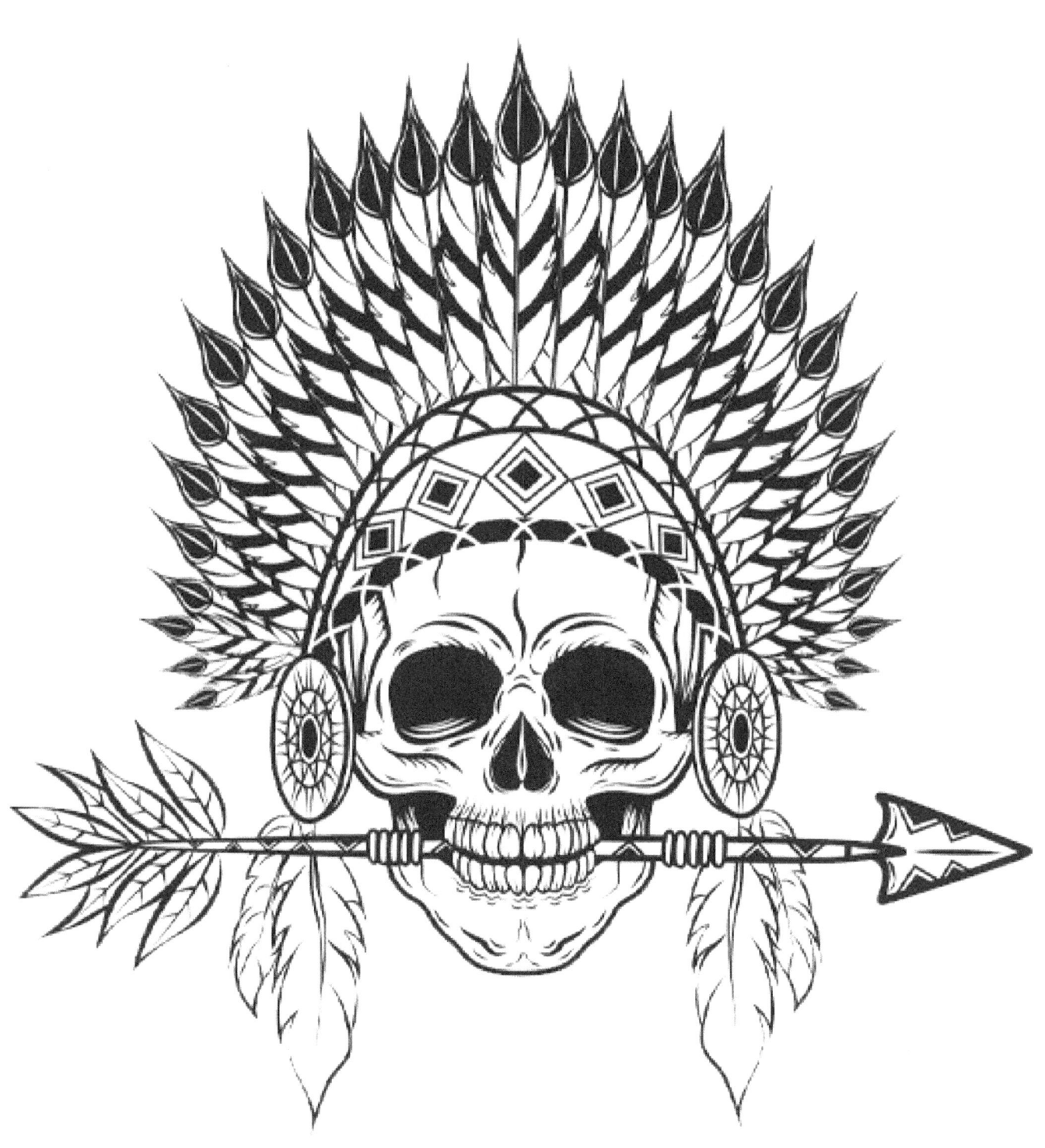

Coloring Test Pages

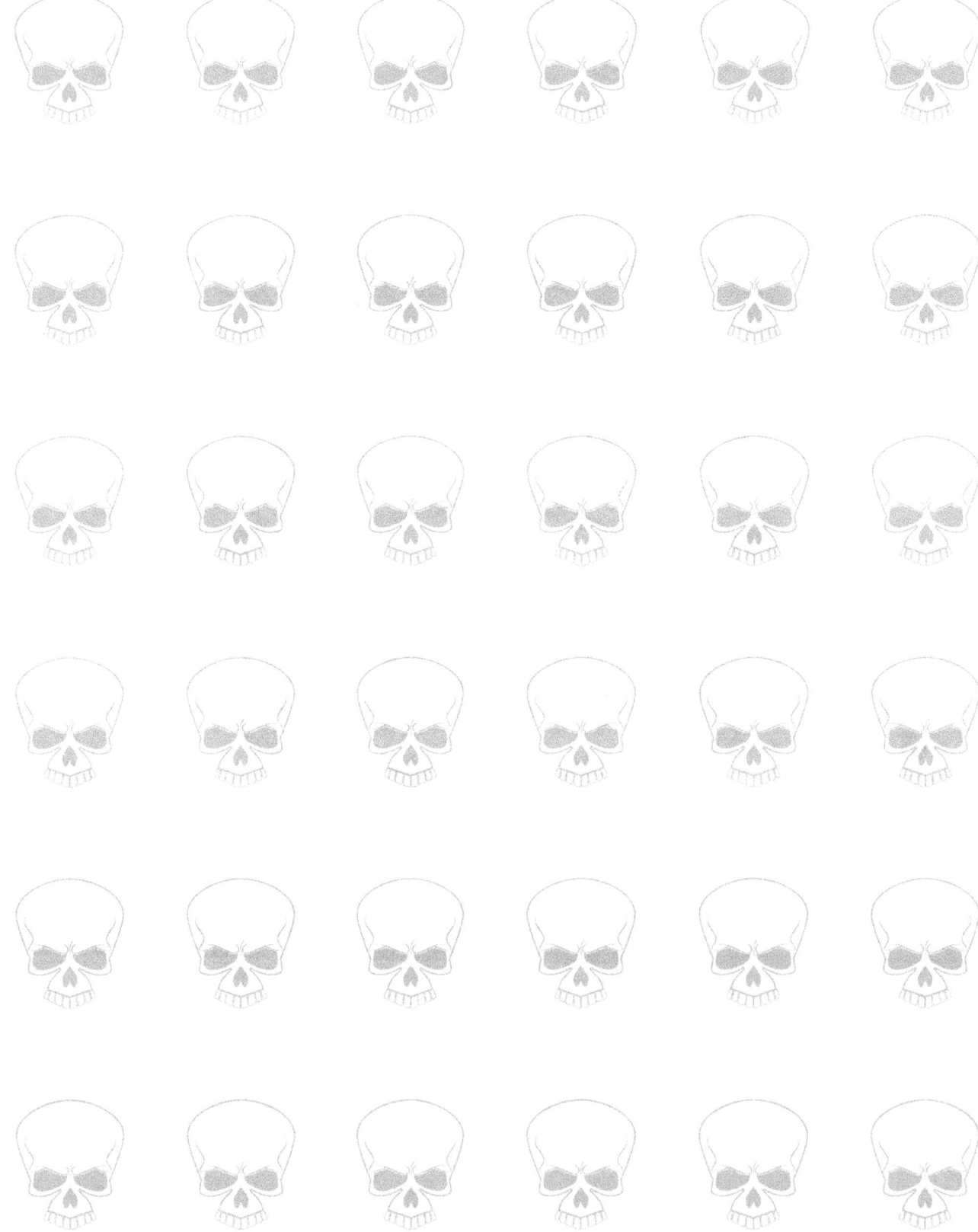

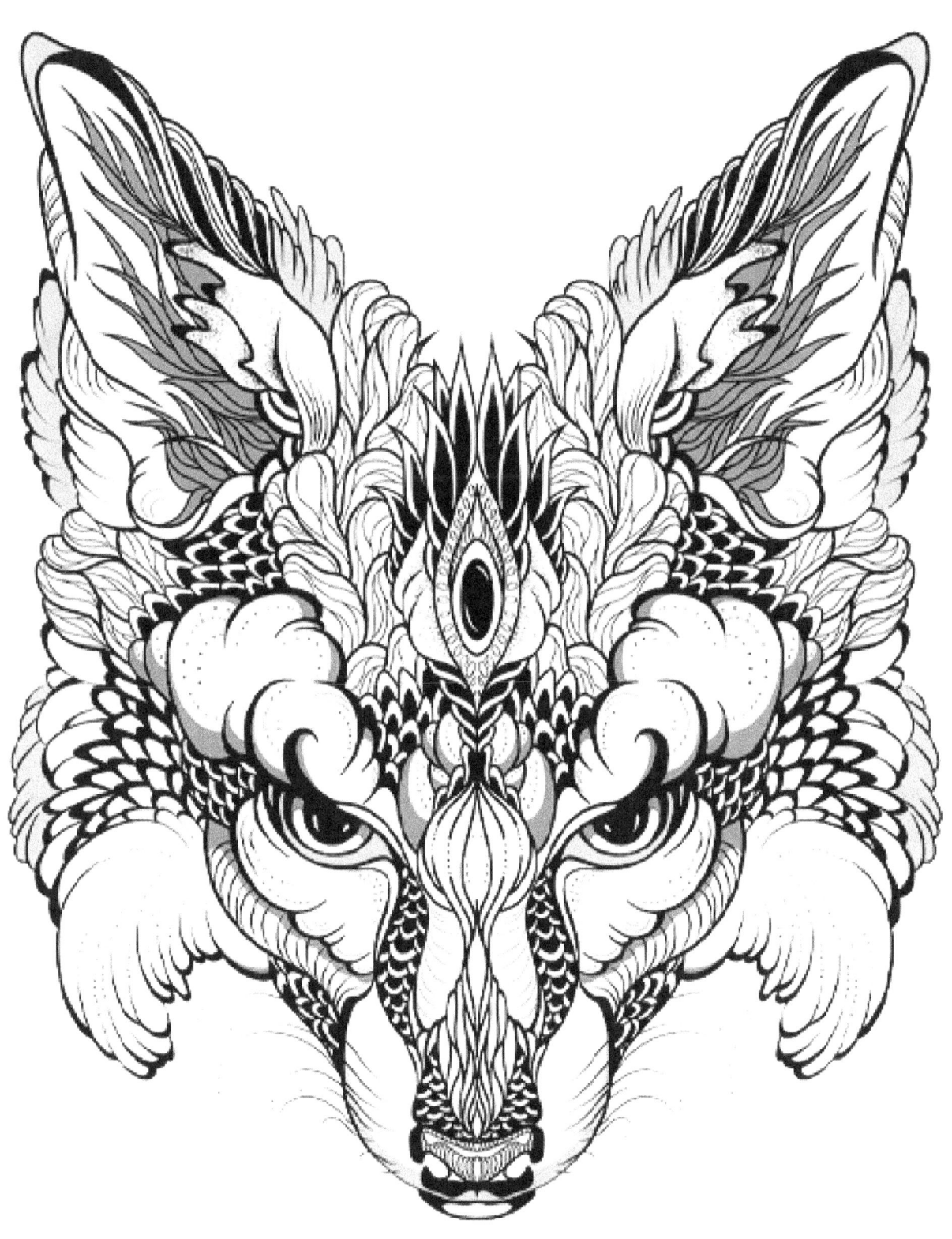

Coloring Test Pages

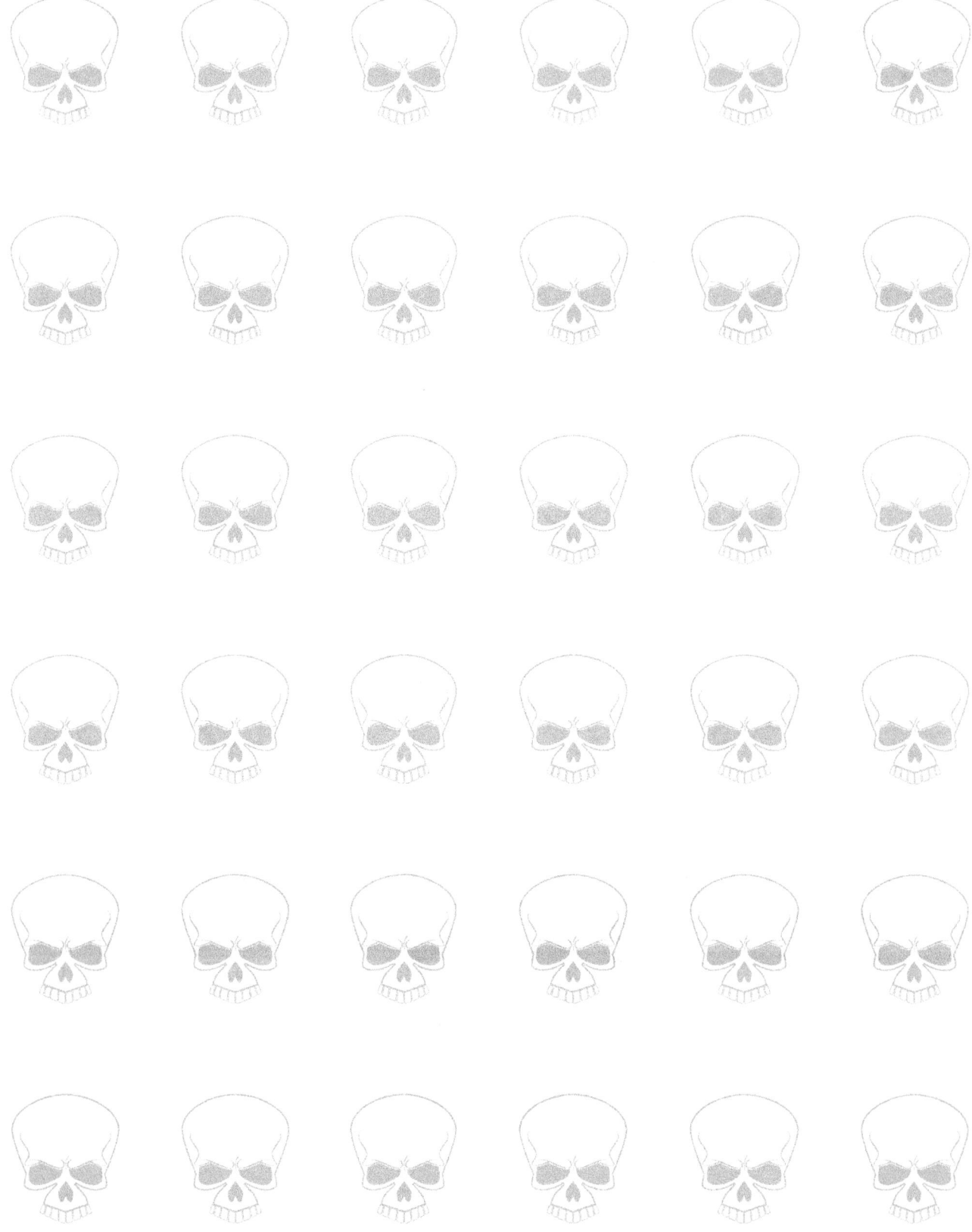

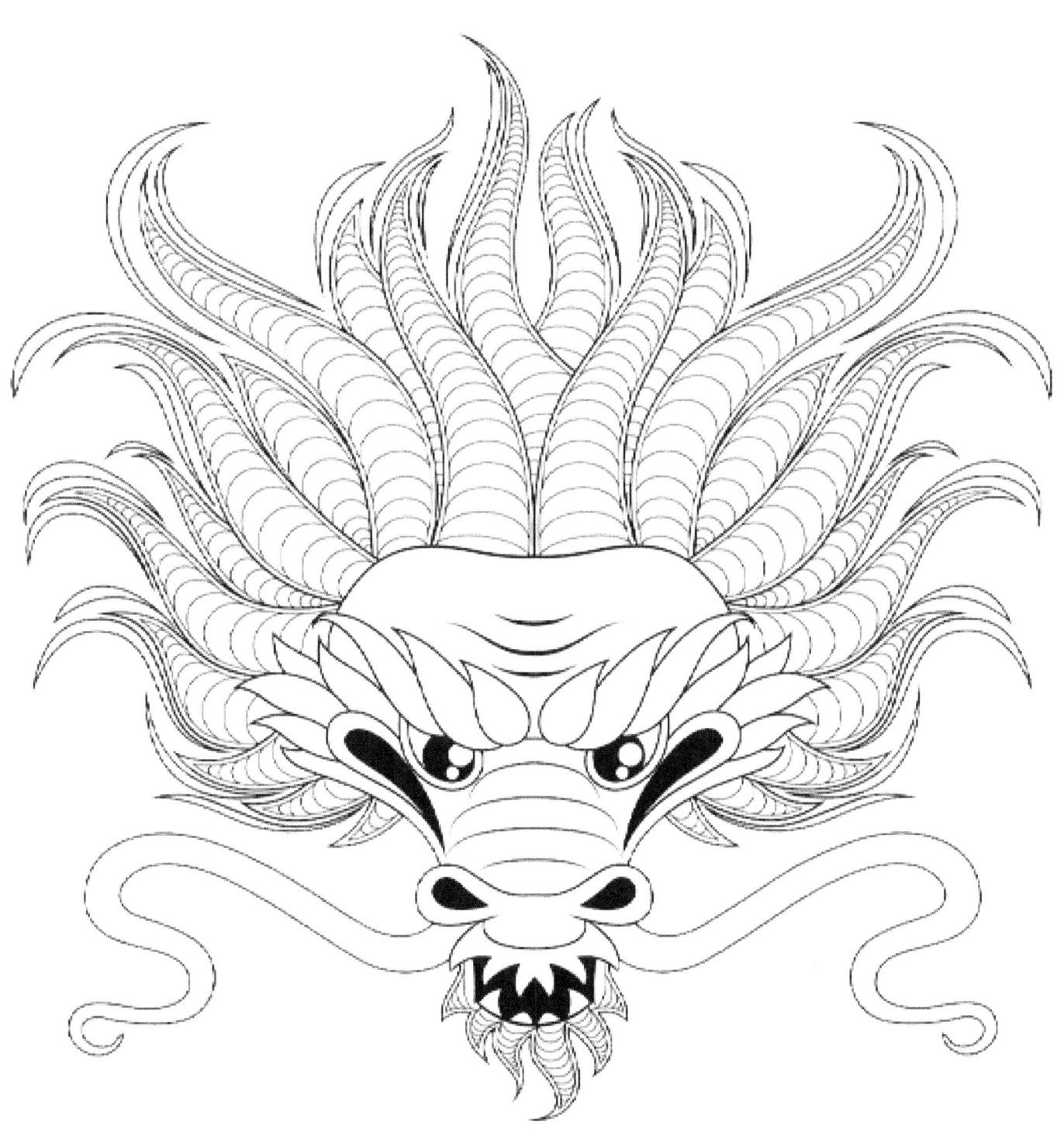

Coloring Test Pages

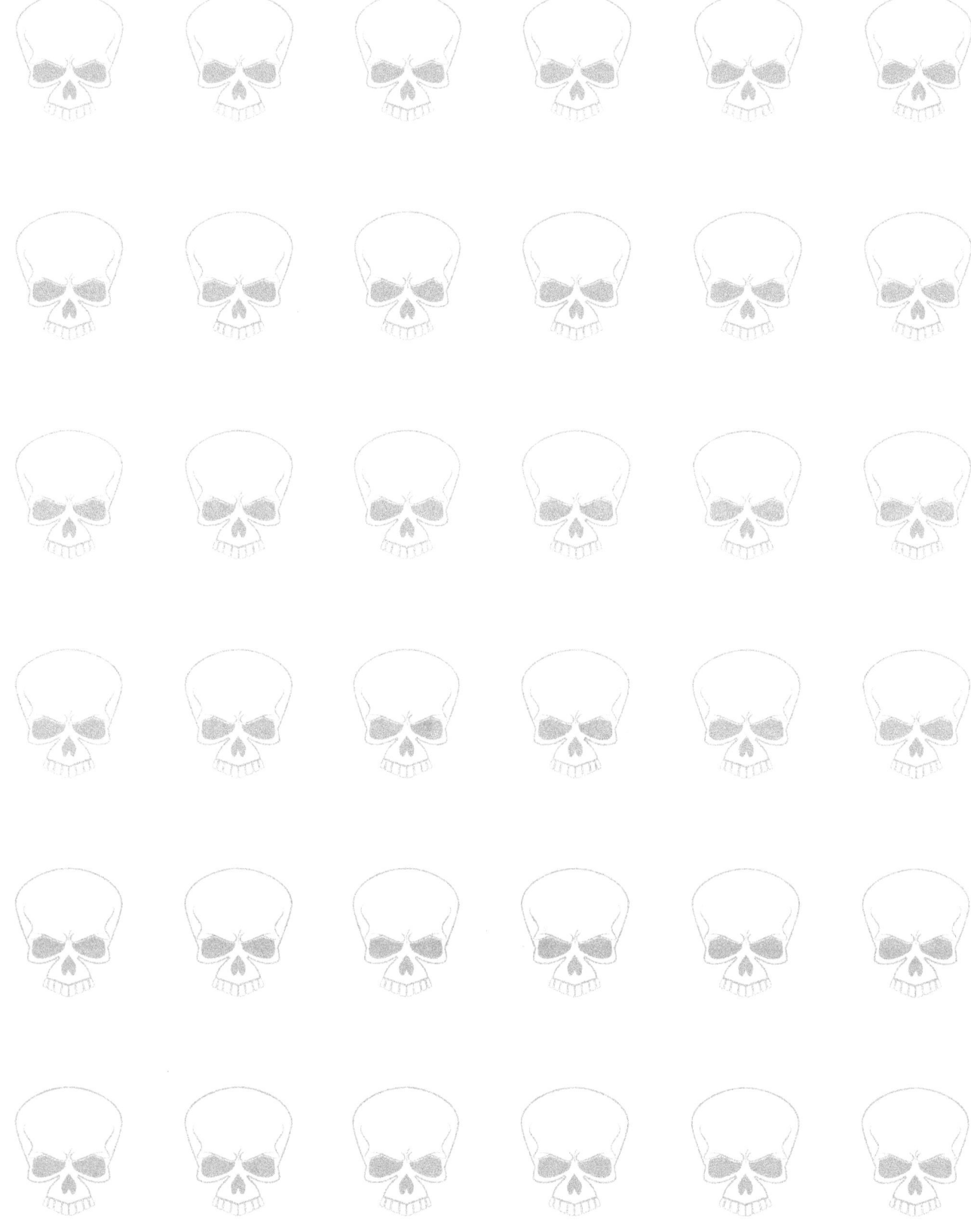

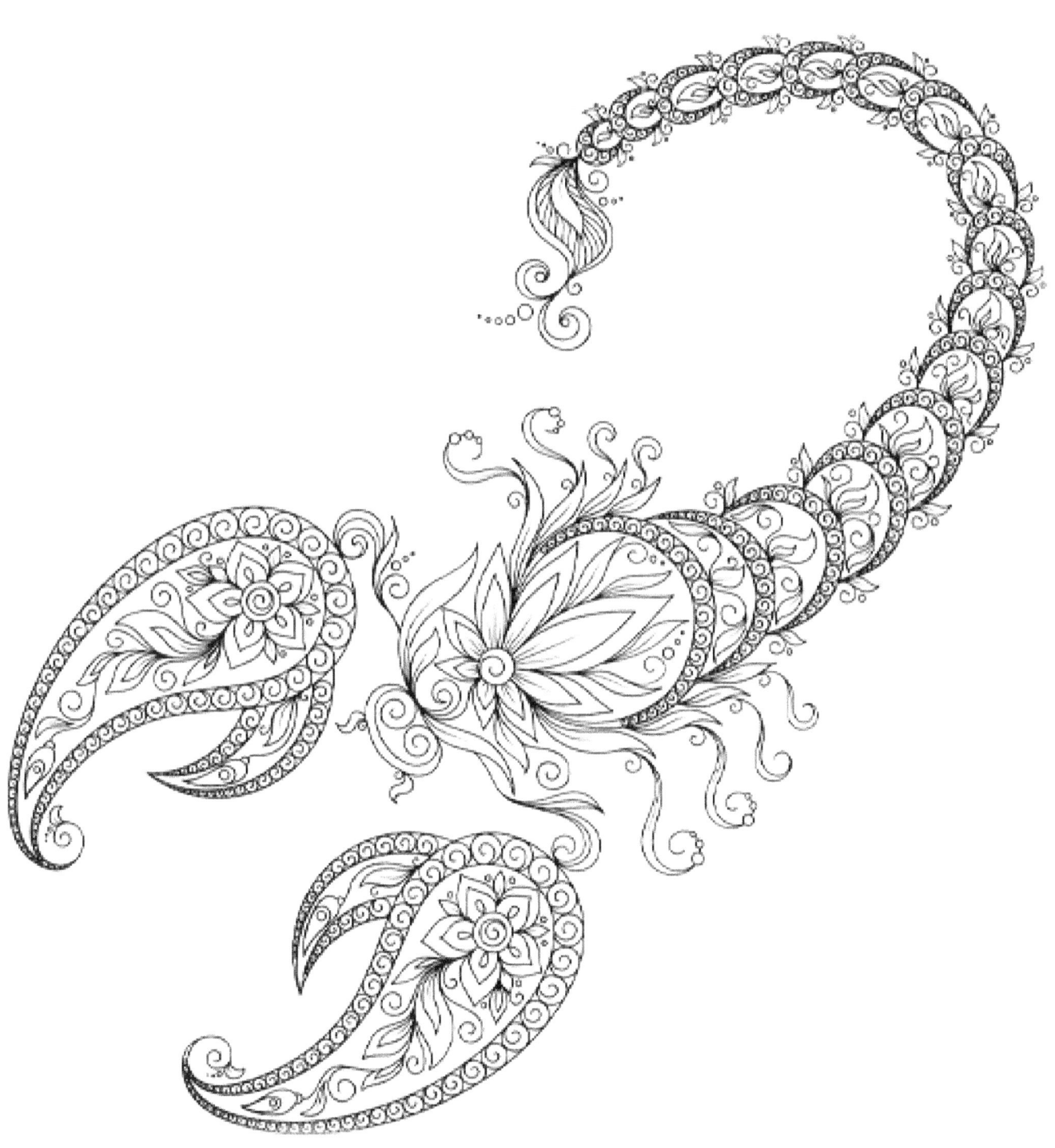

Coloring Test Pages

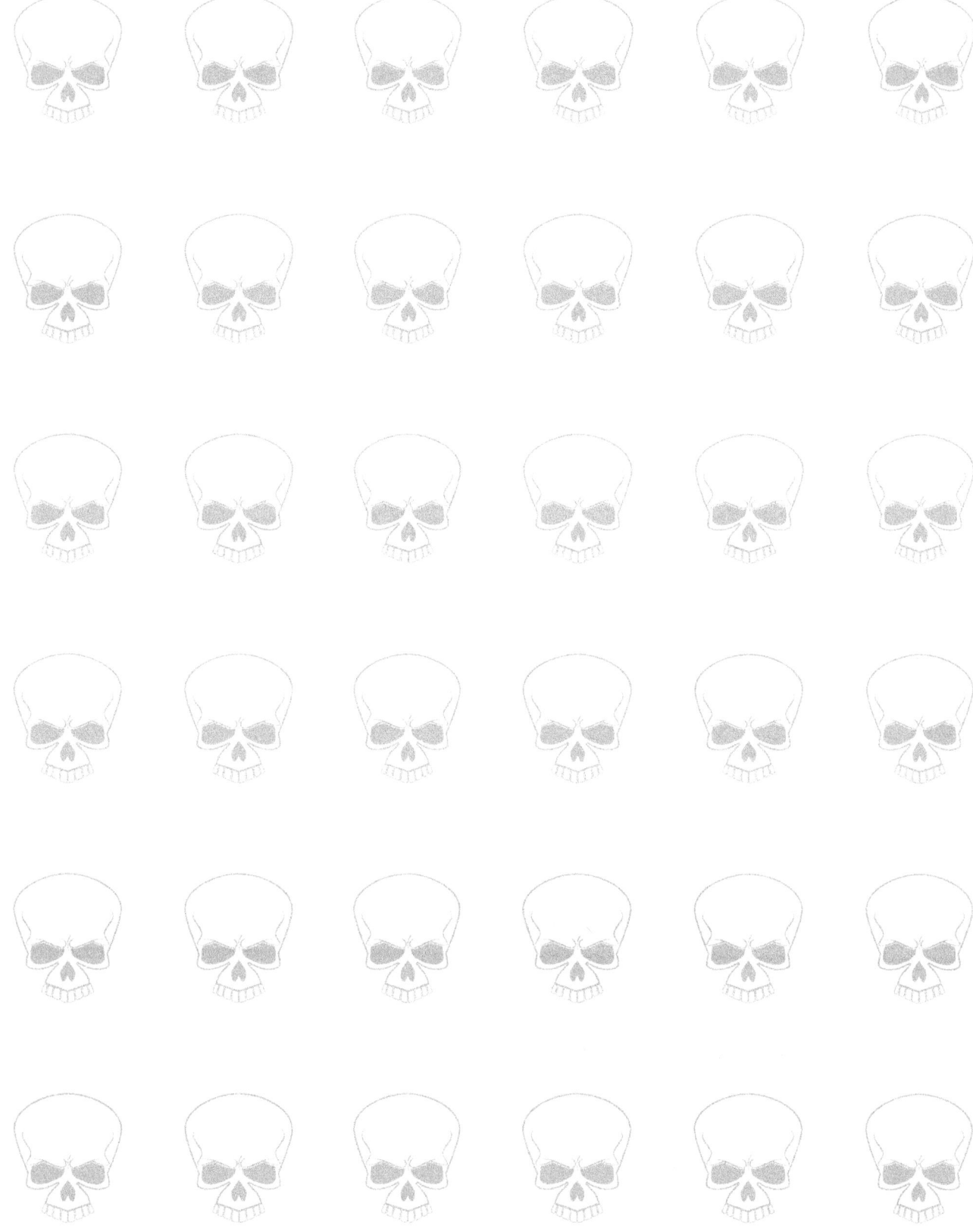

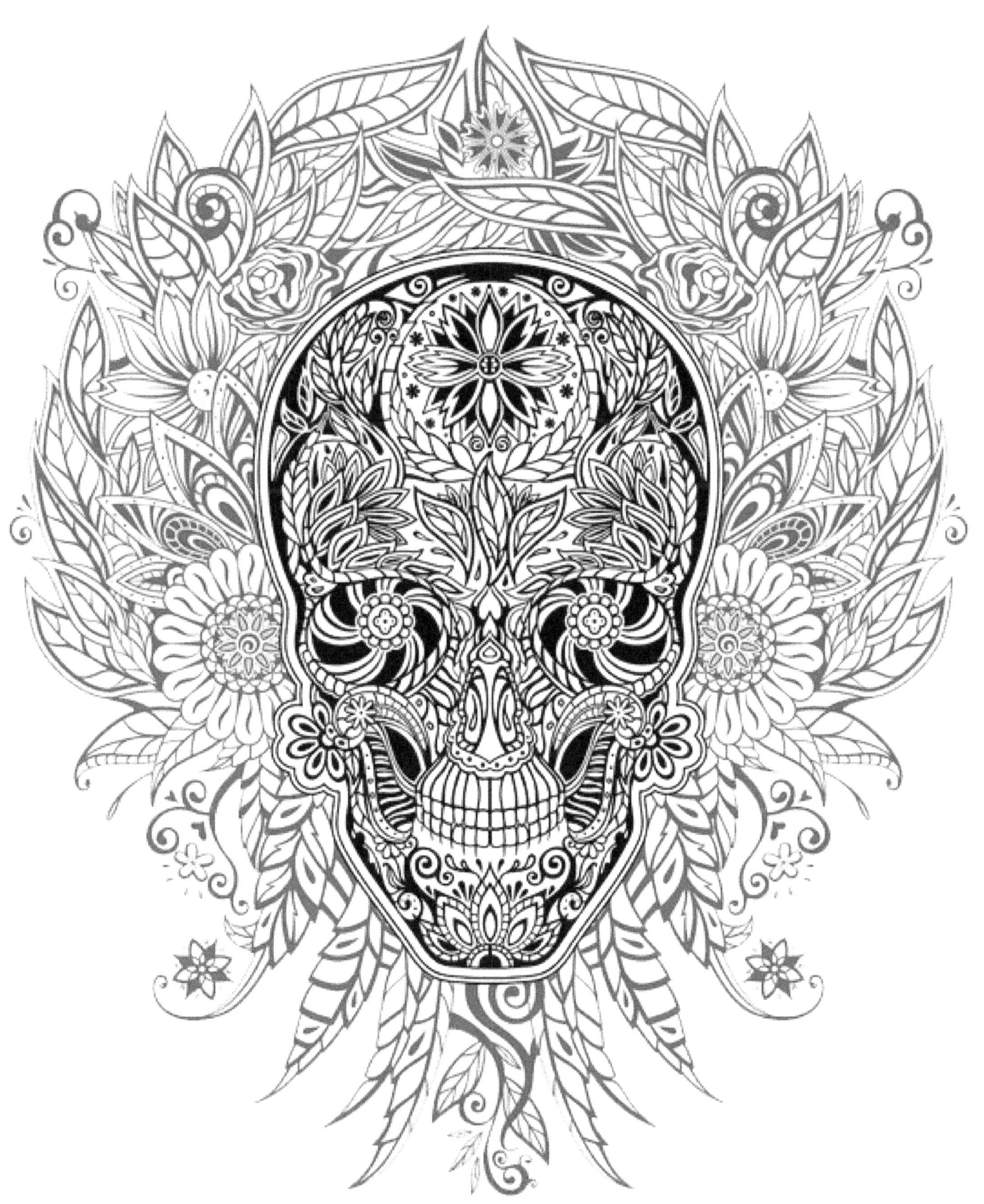

Coloring Test Pages

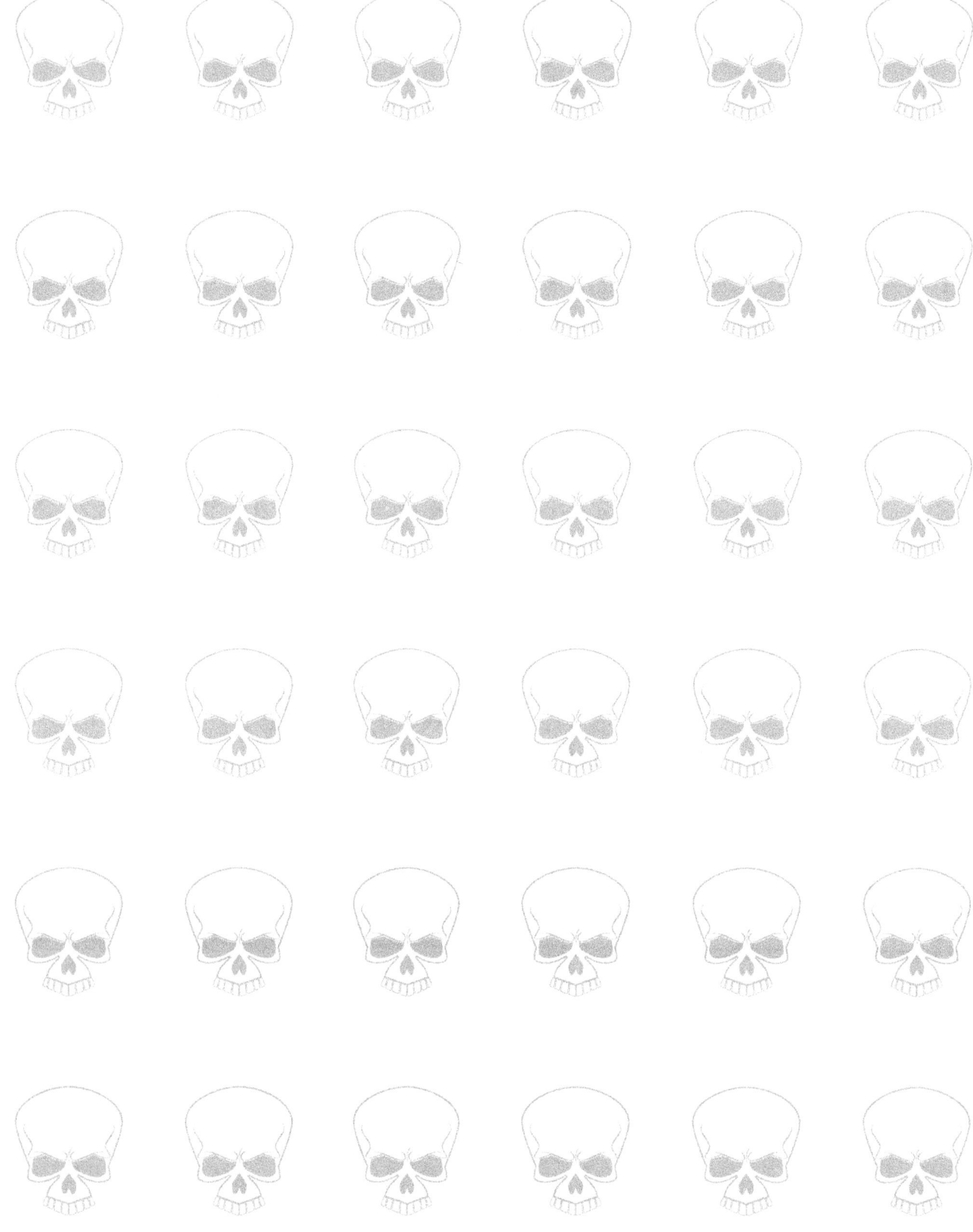

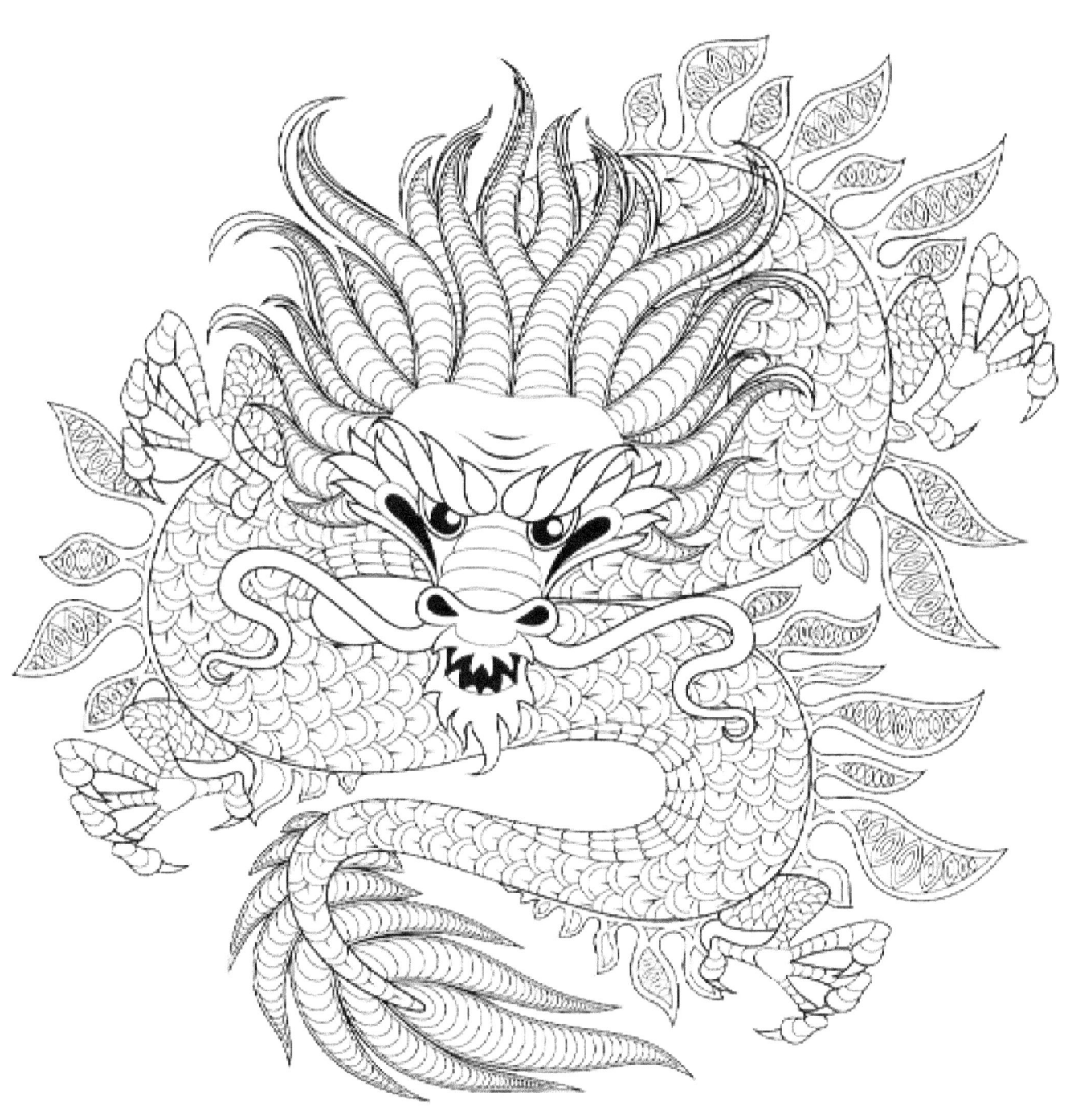

Coloring Test Pages

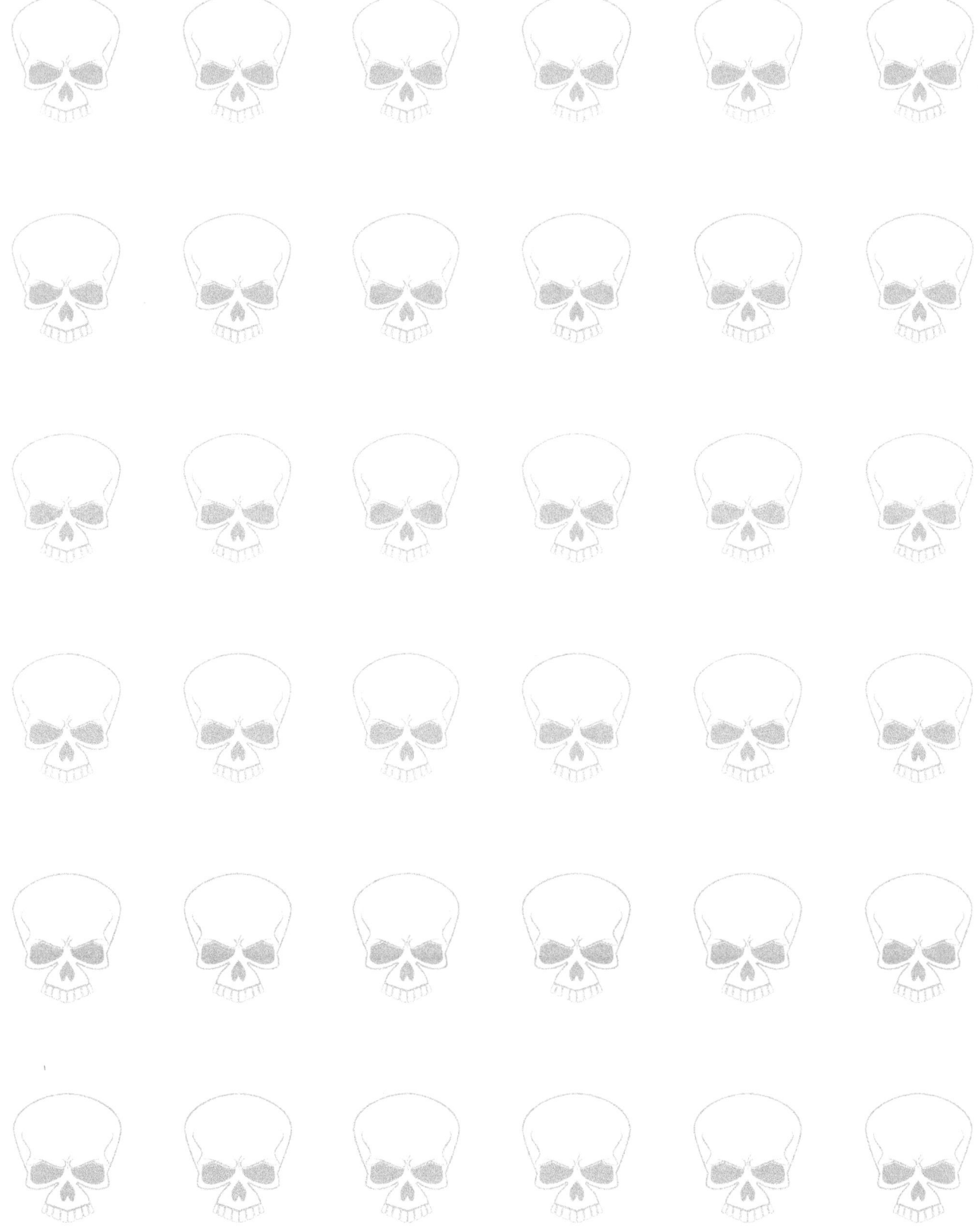

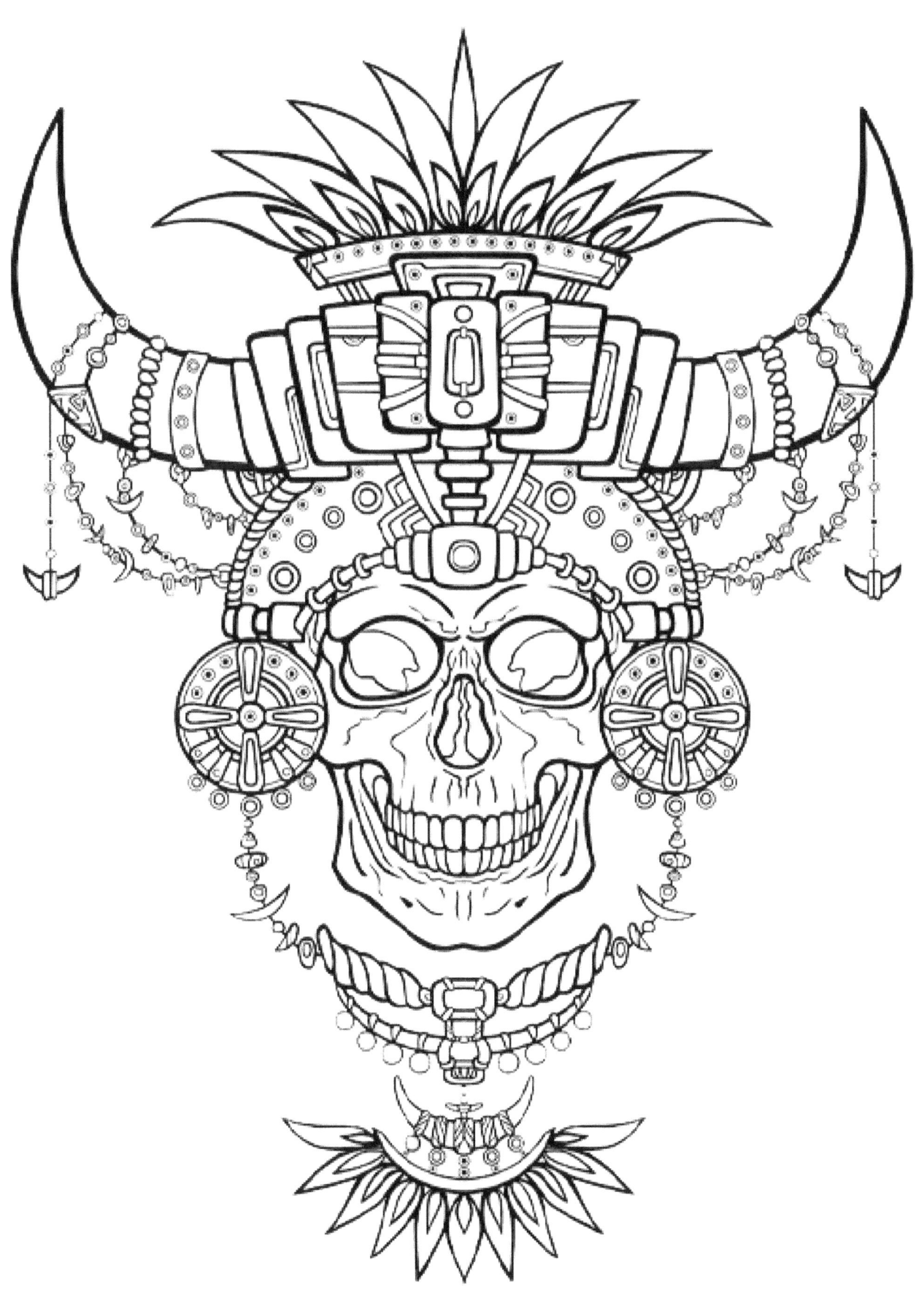

Coloring Test Pages

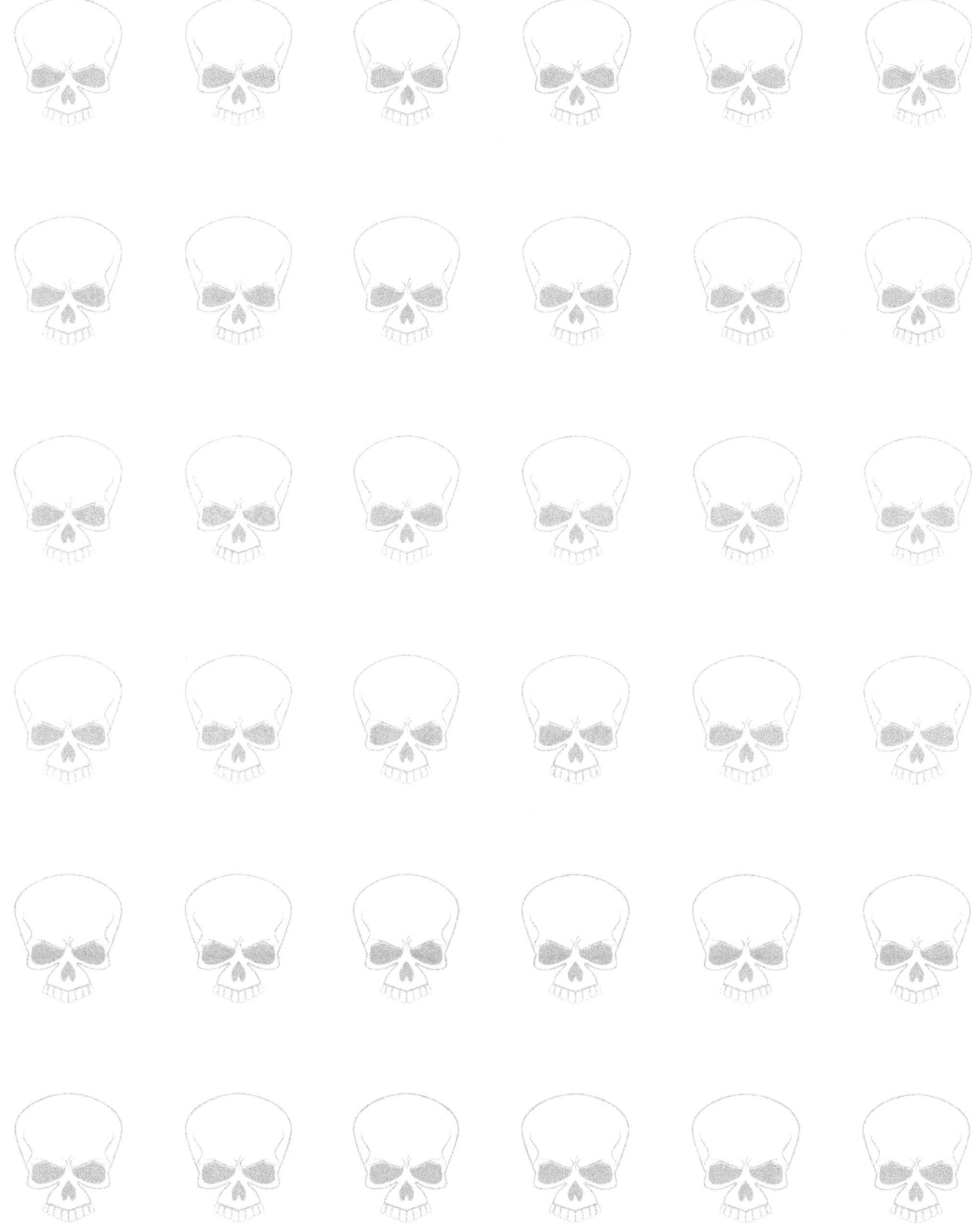

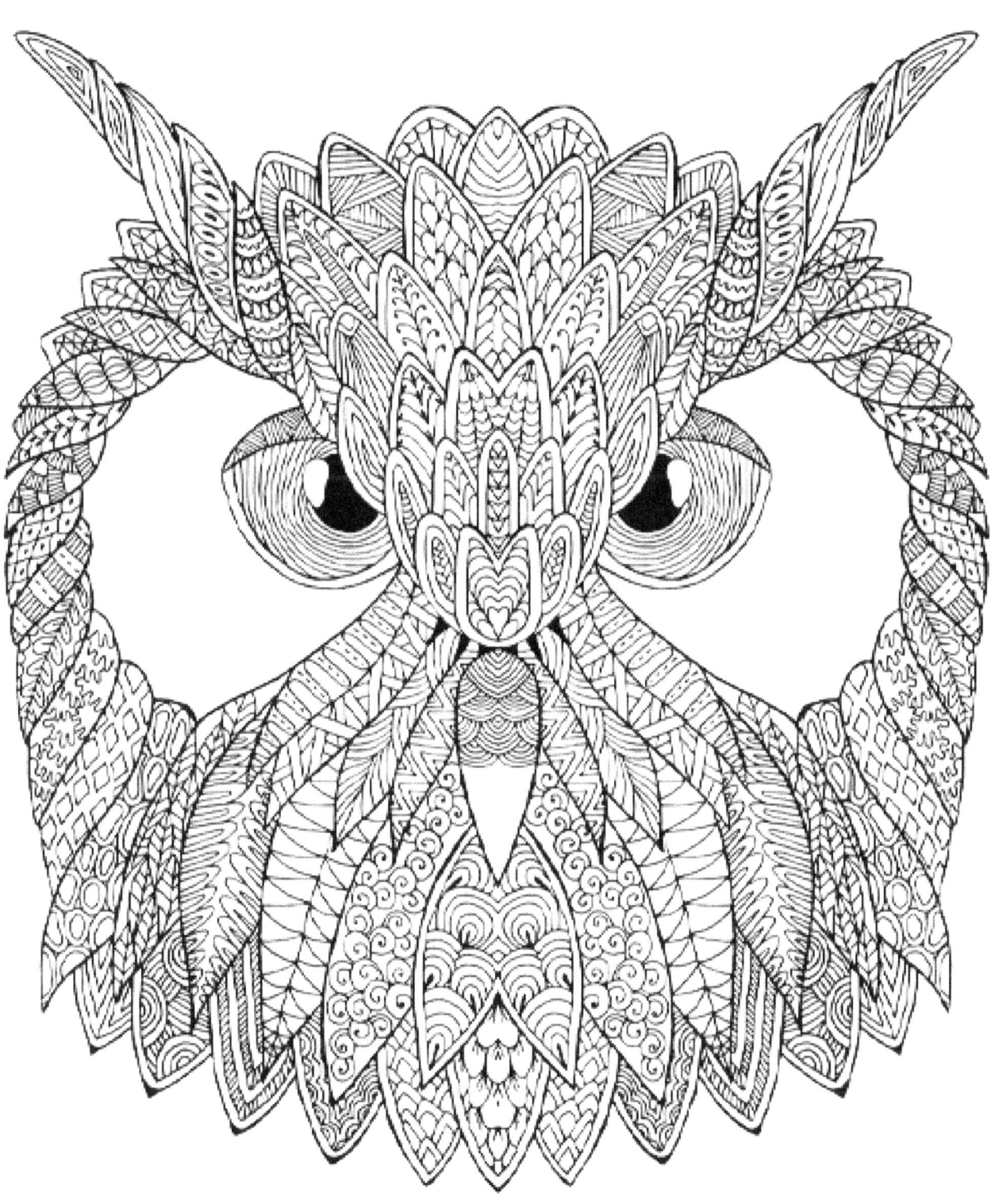

Coloring Test Pages

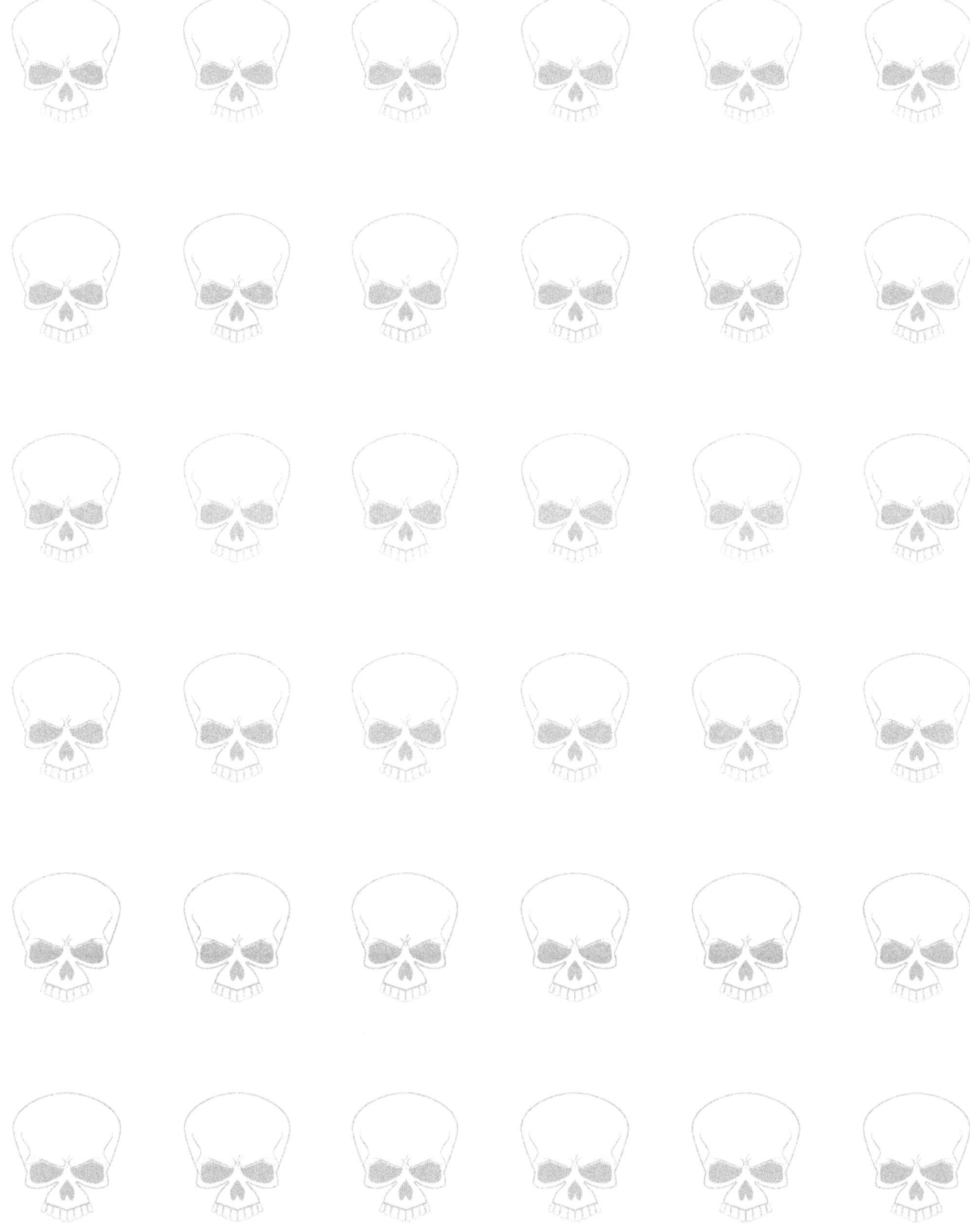

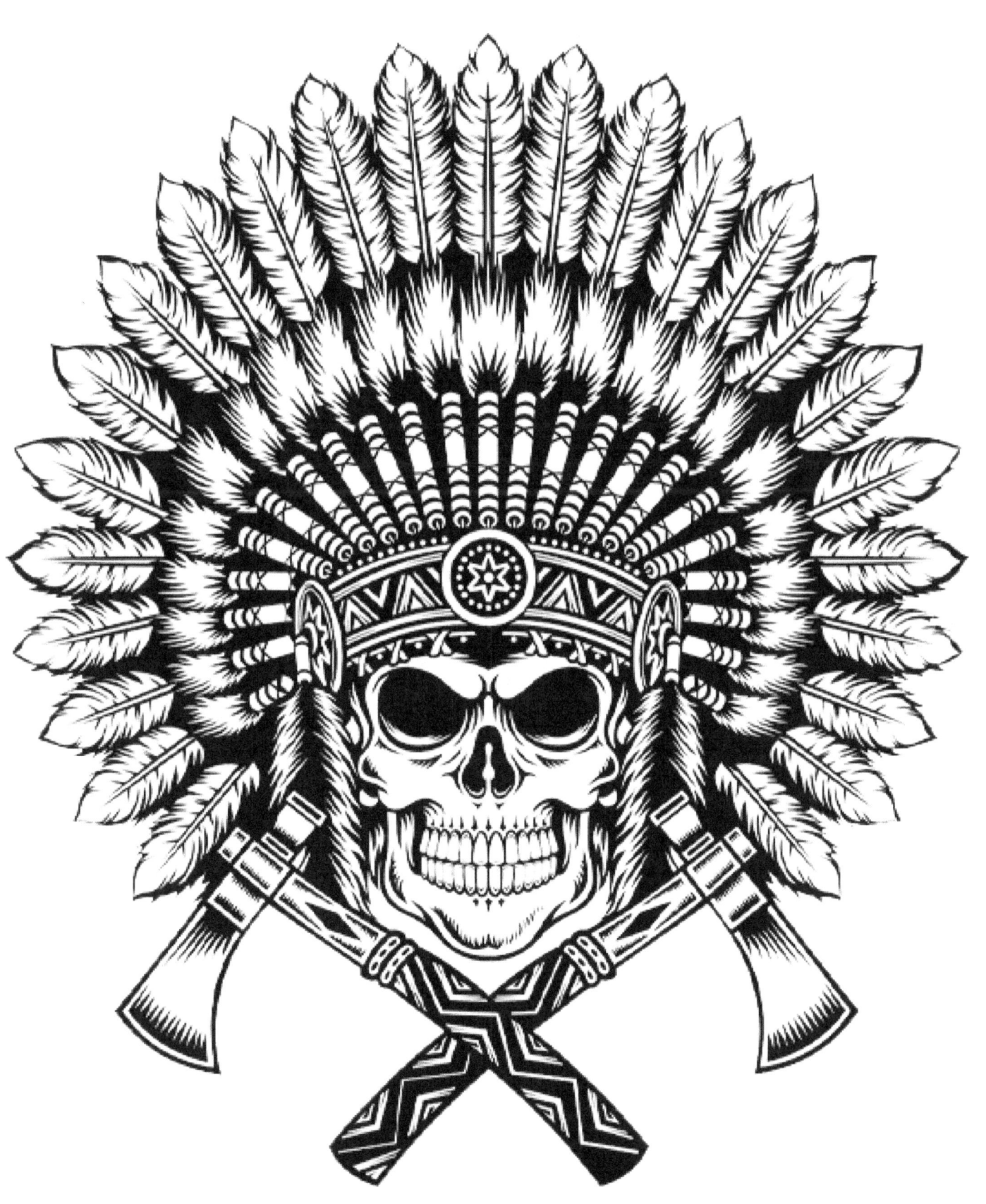

Coloring Test Pages

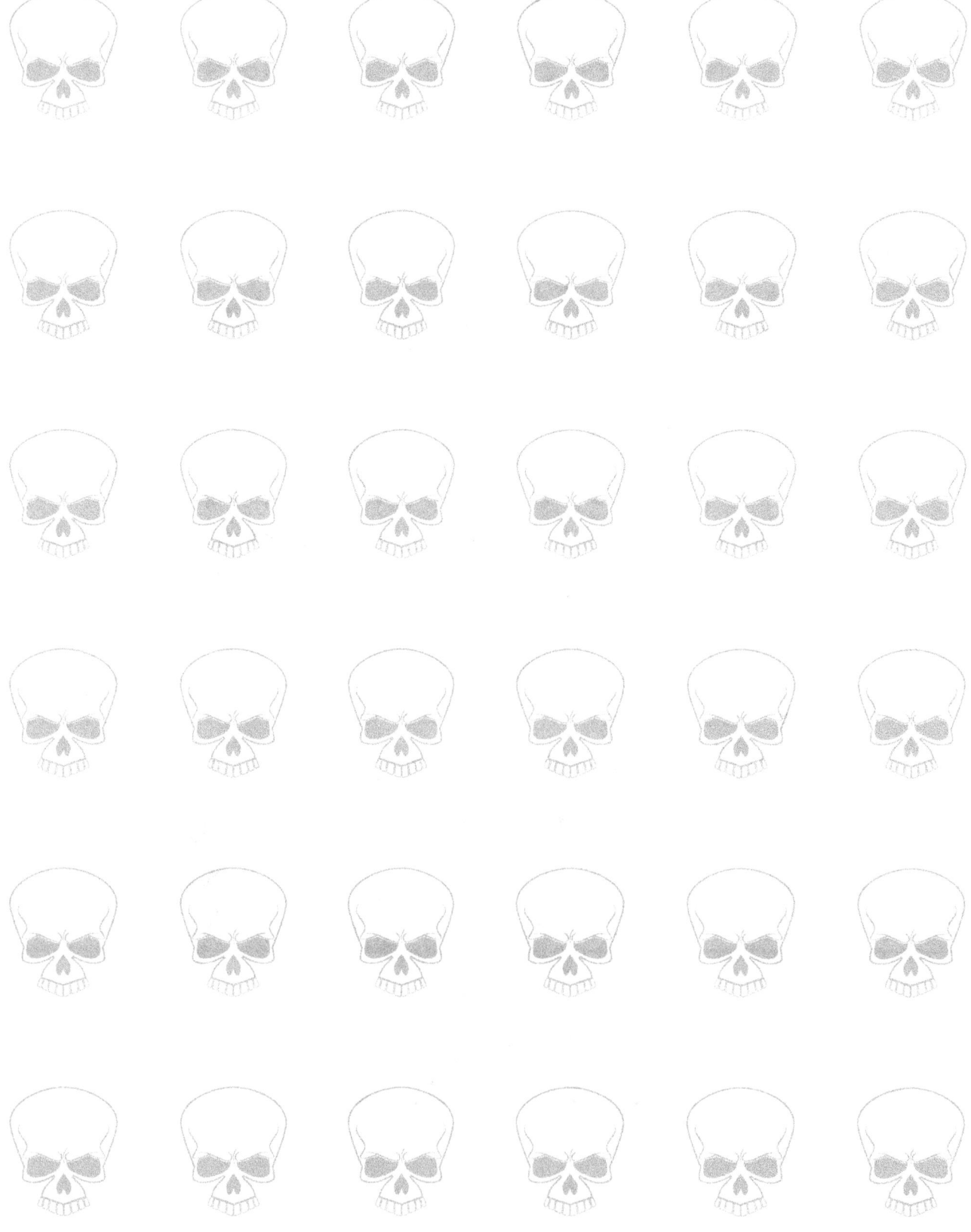

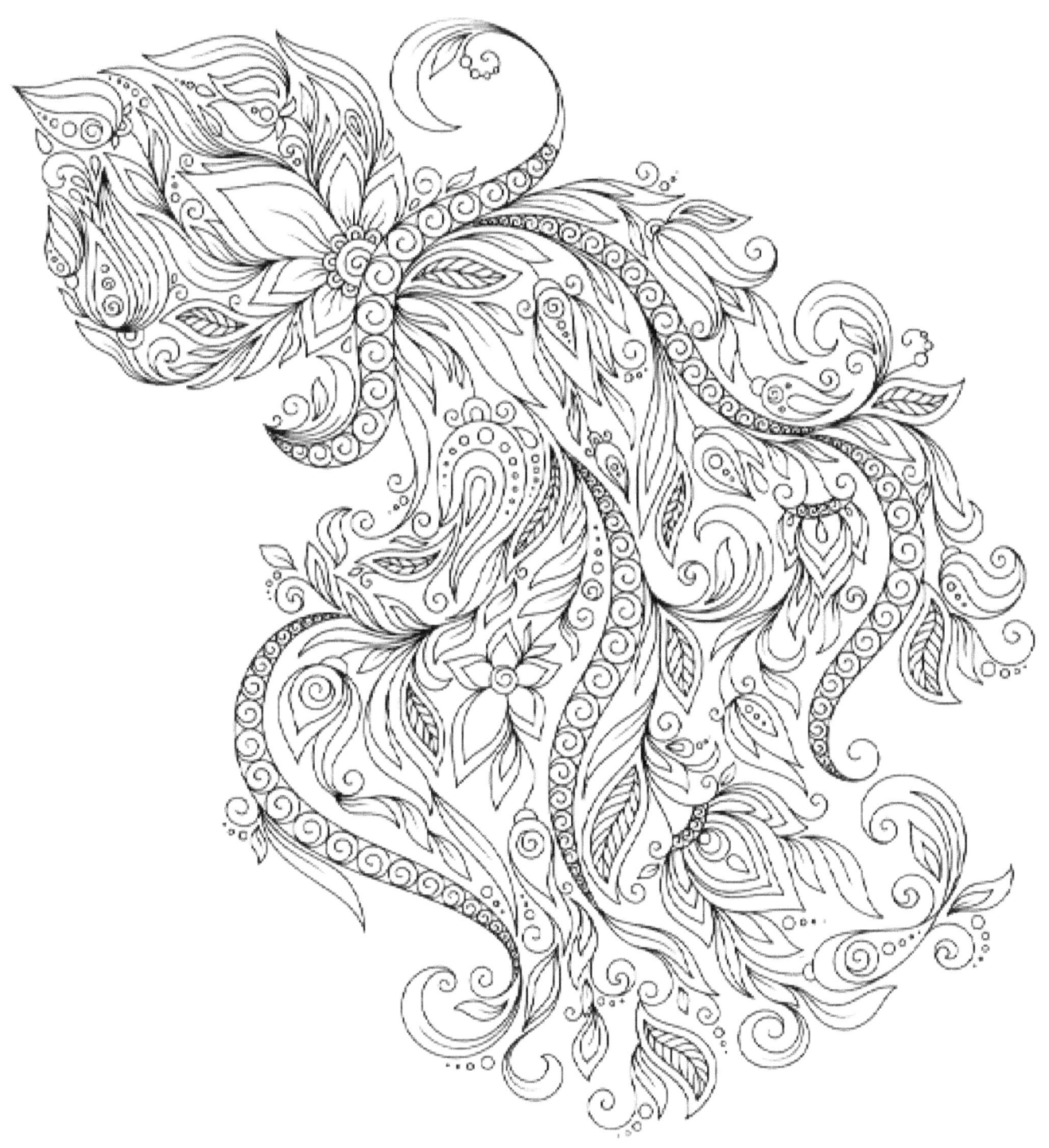

Coloring Test Pages

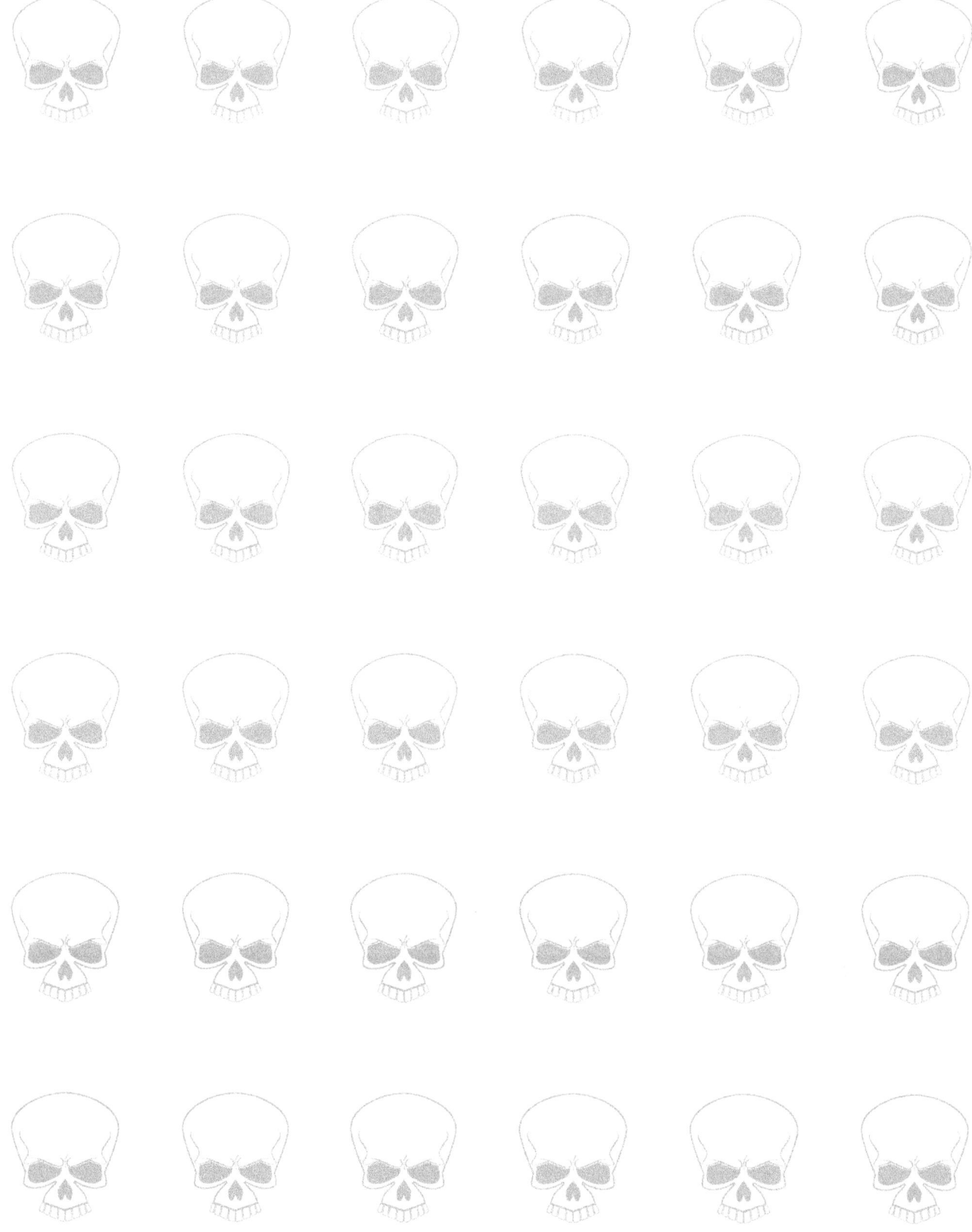

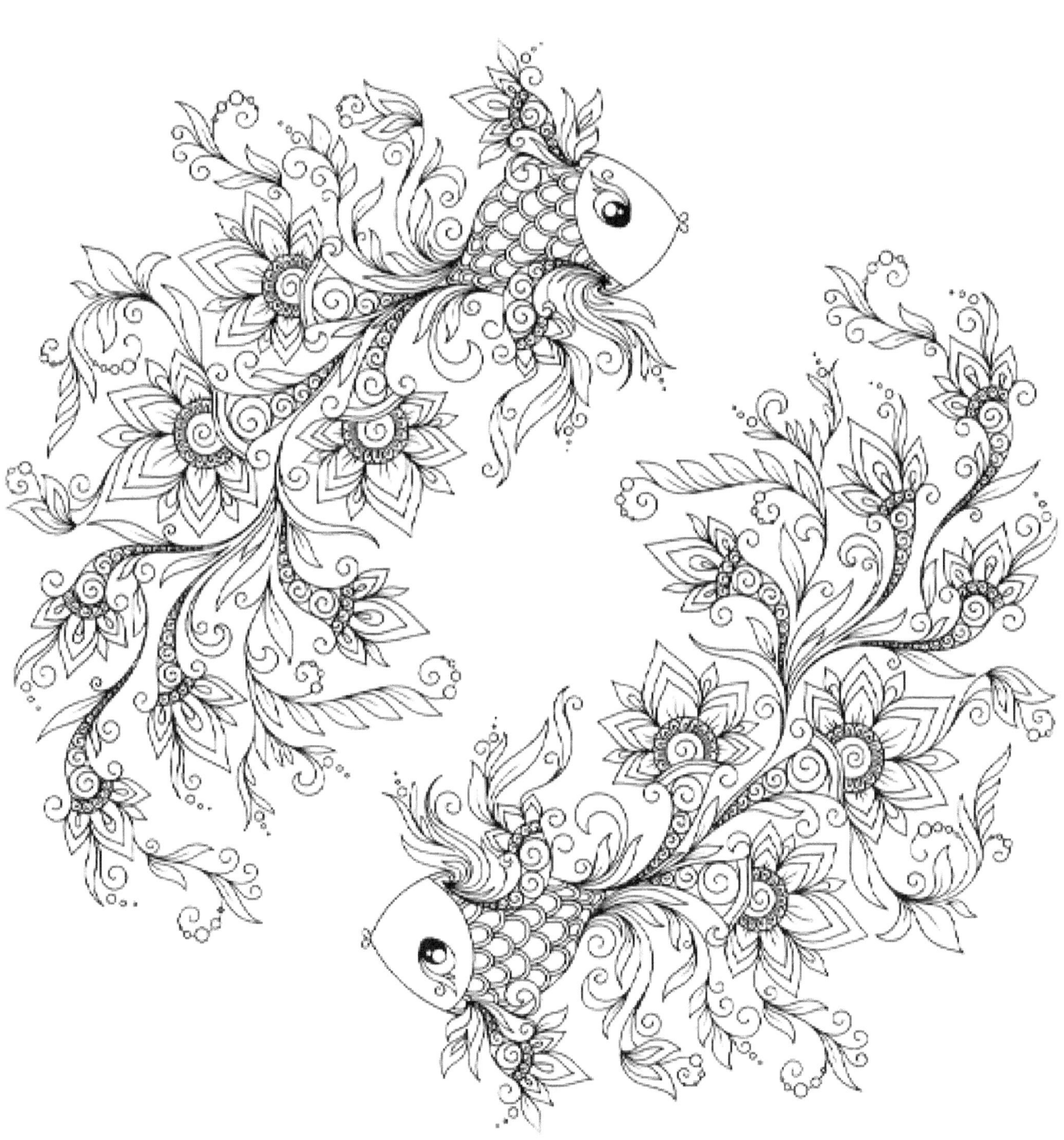

Coloring Test Pages

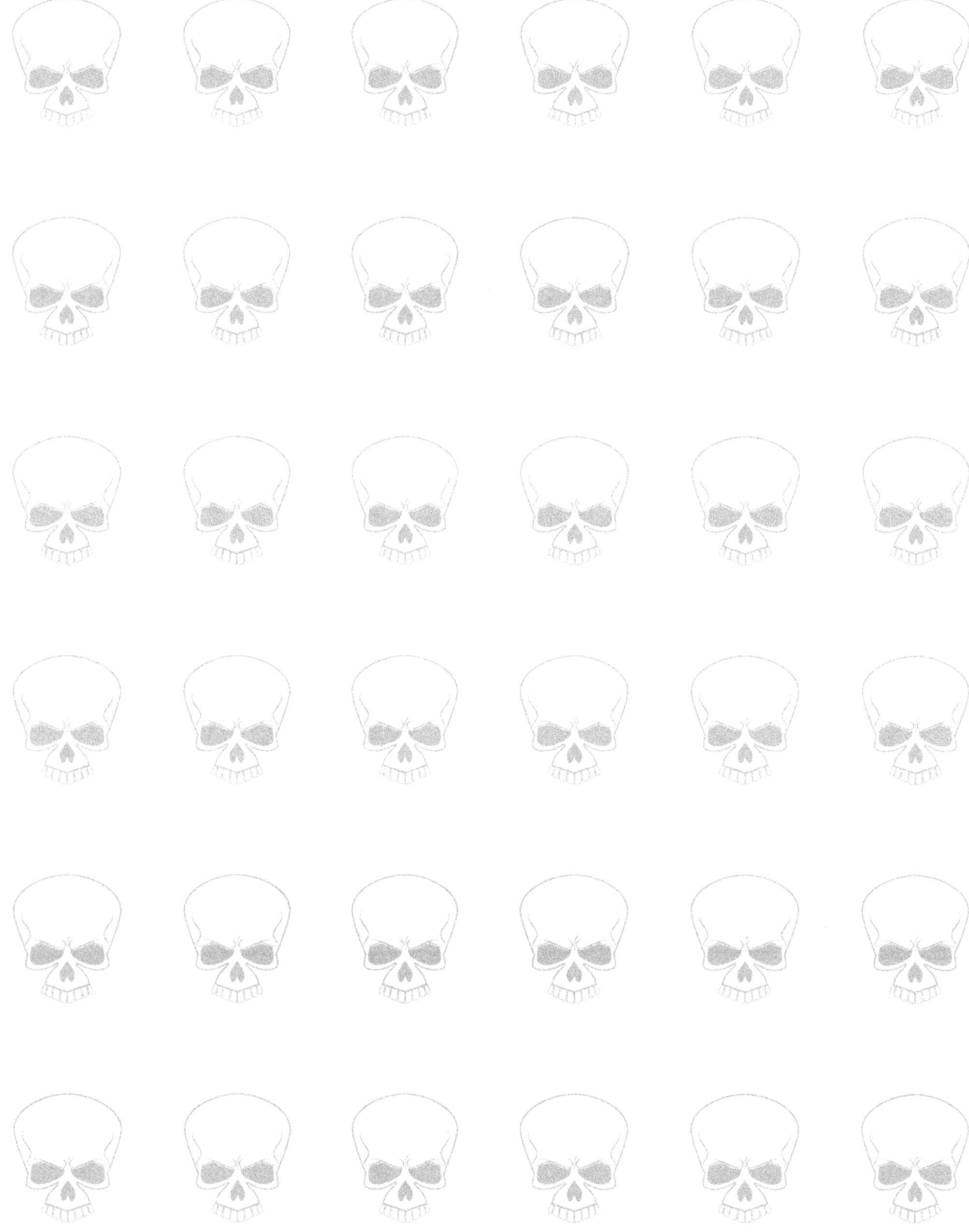

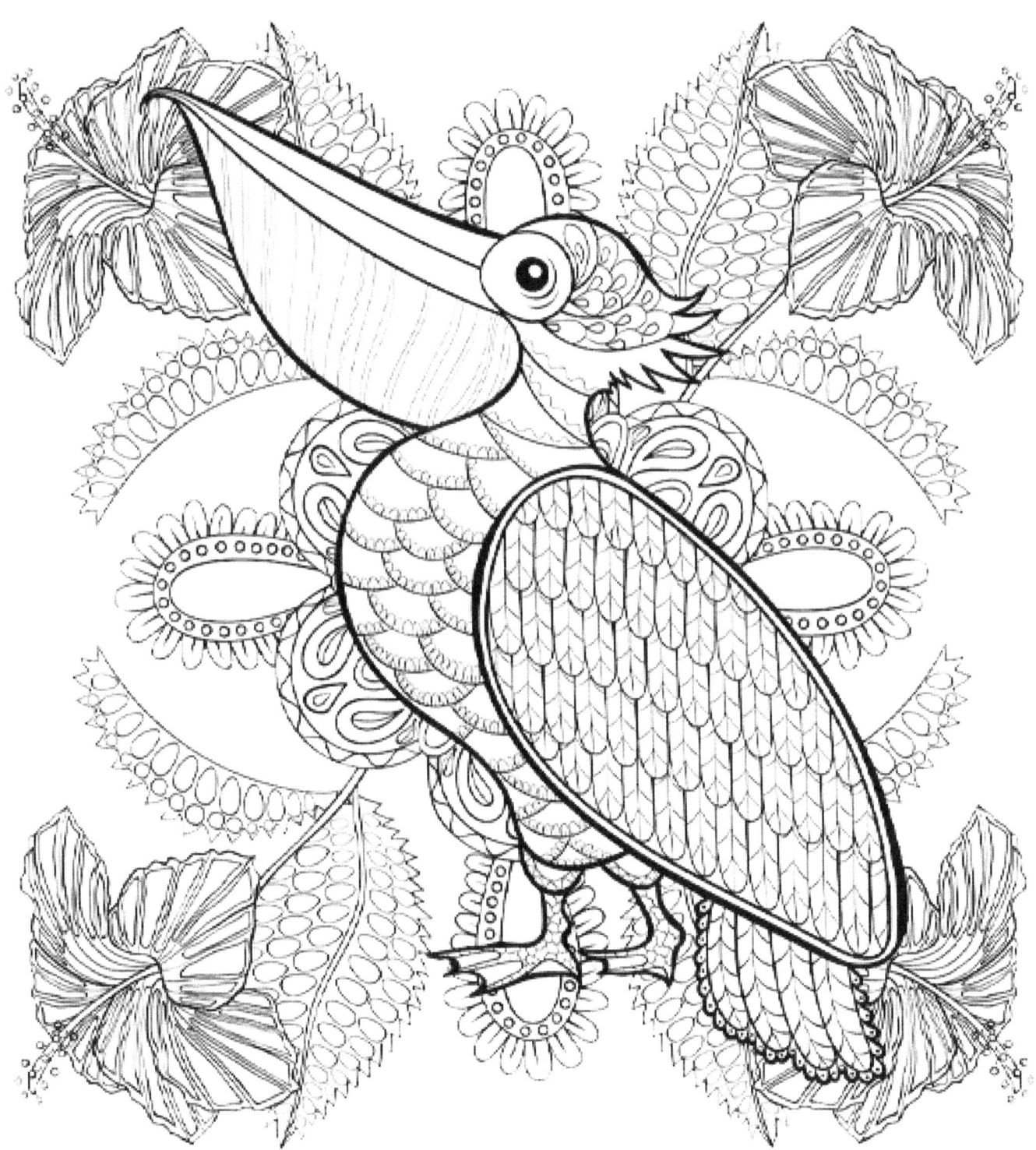

Coloring Test Pages

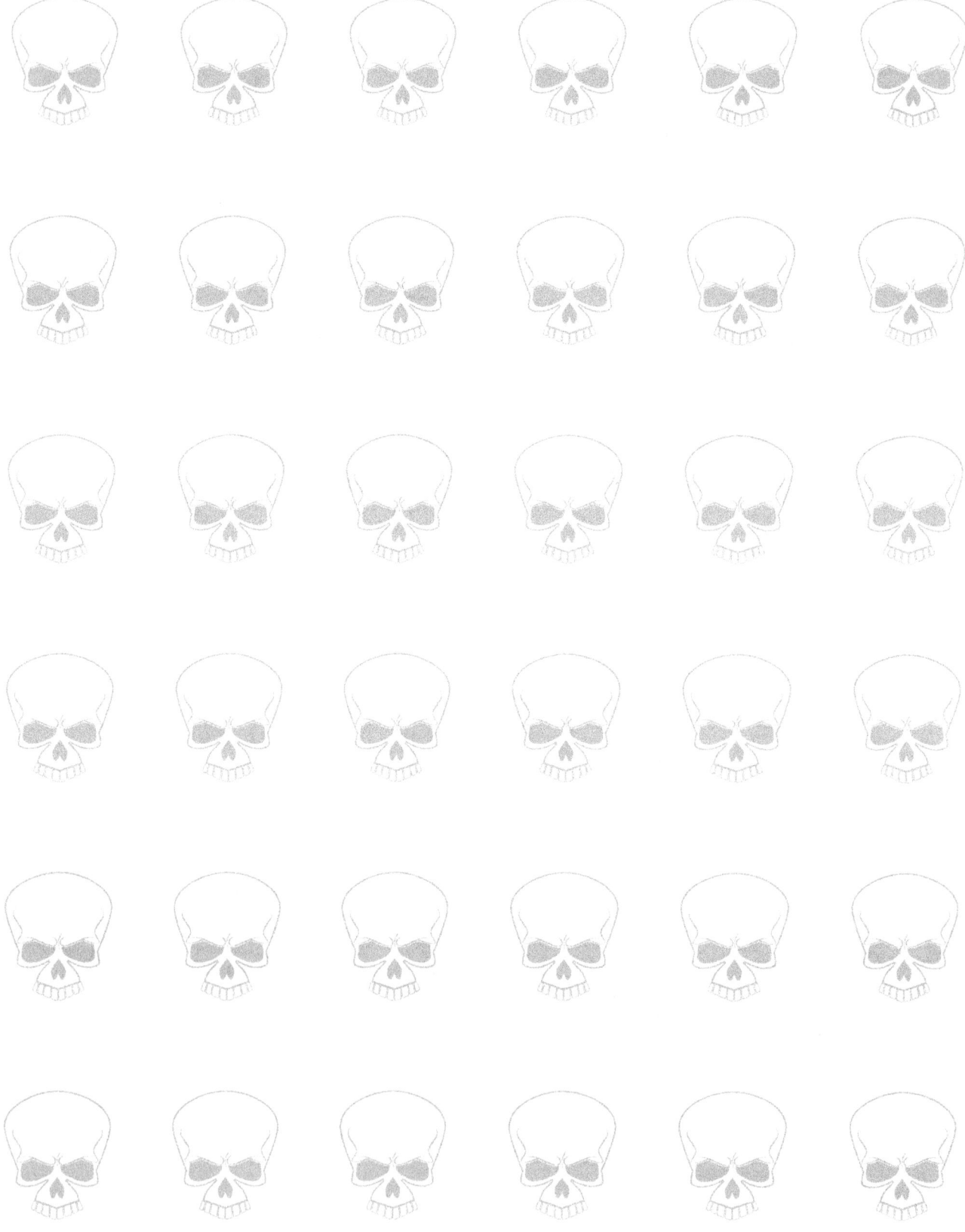

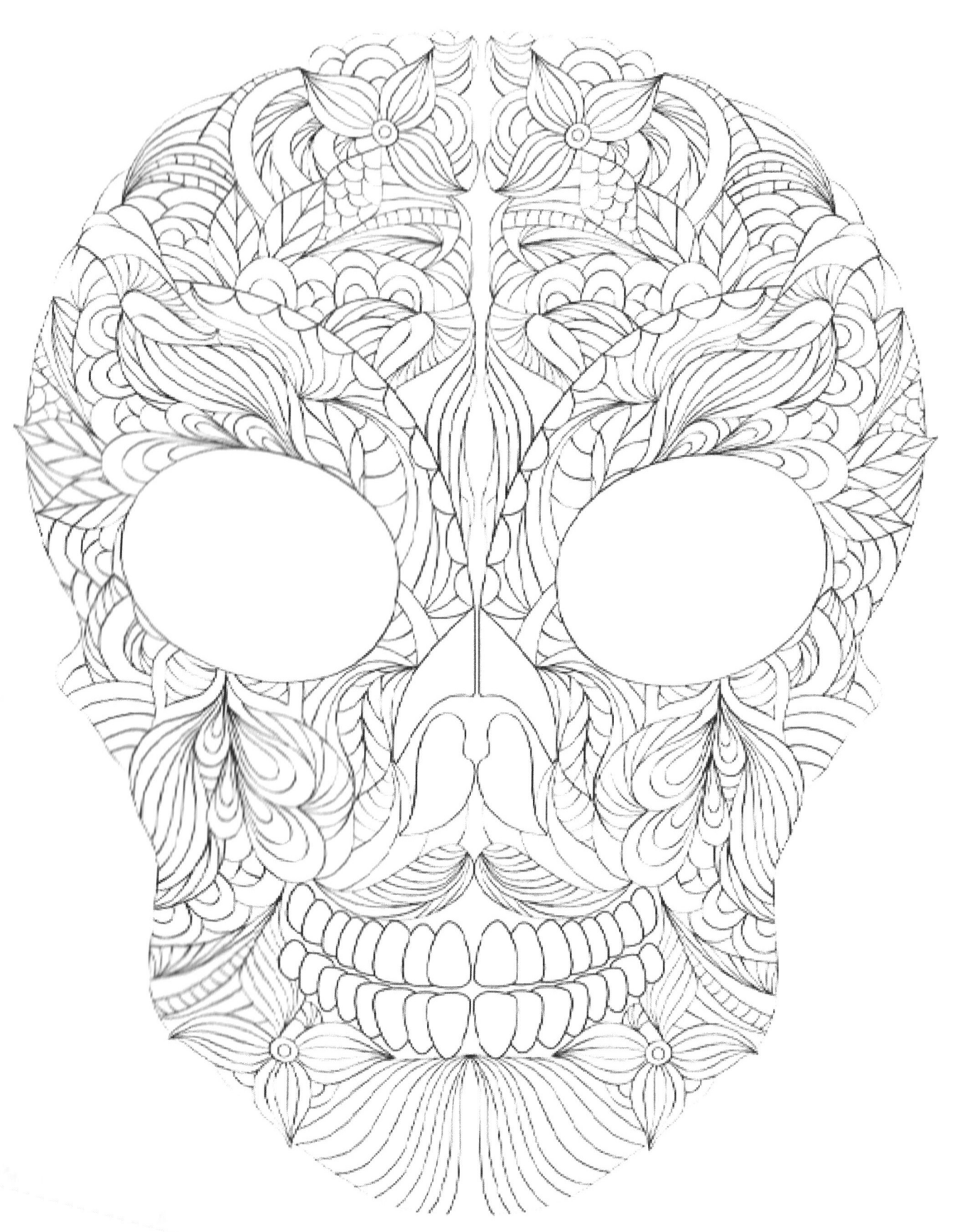

Coloring Test Pages

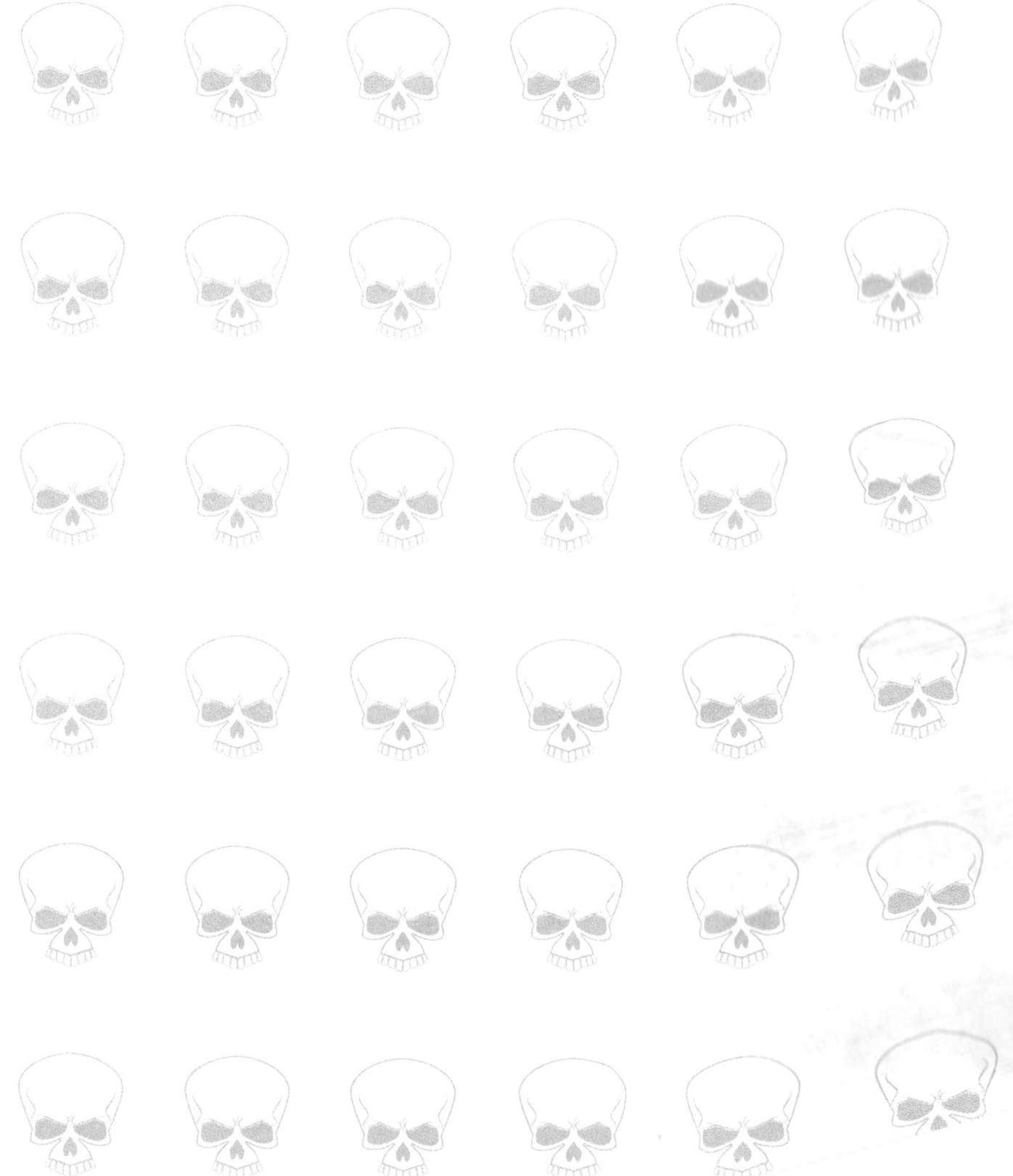

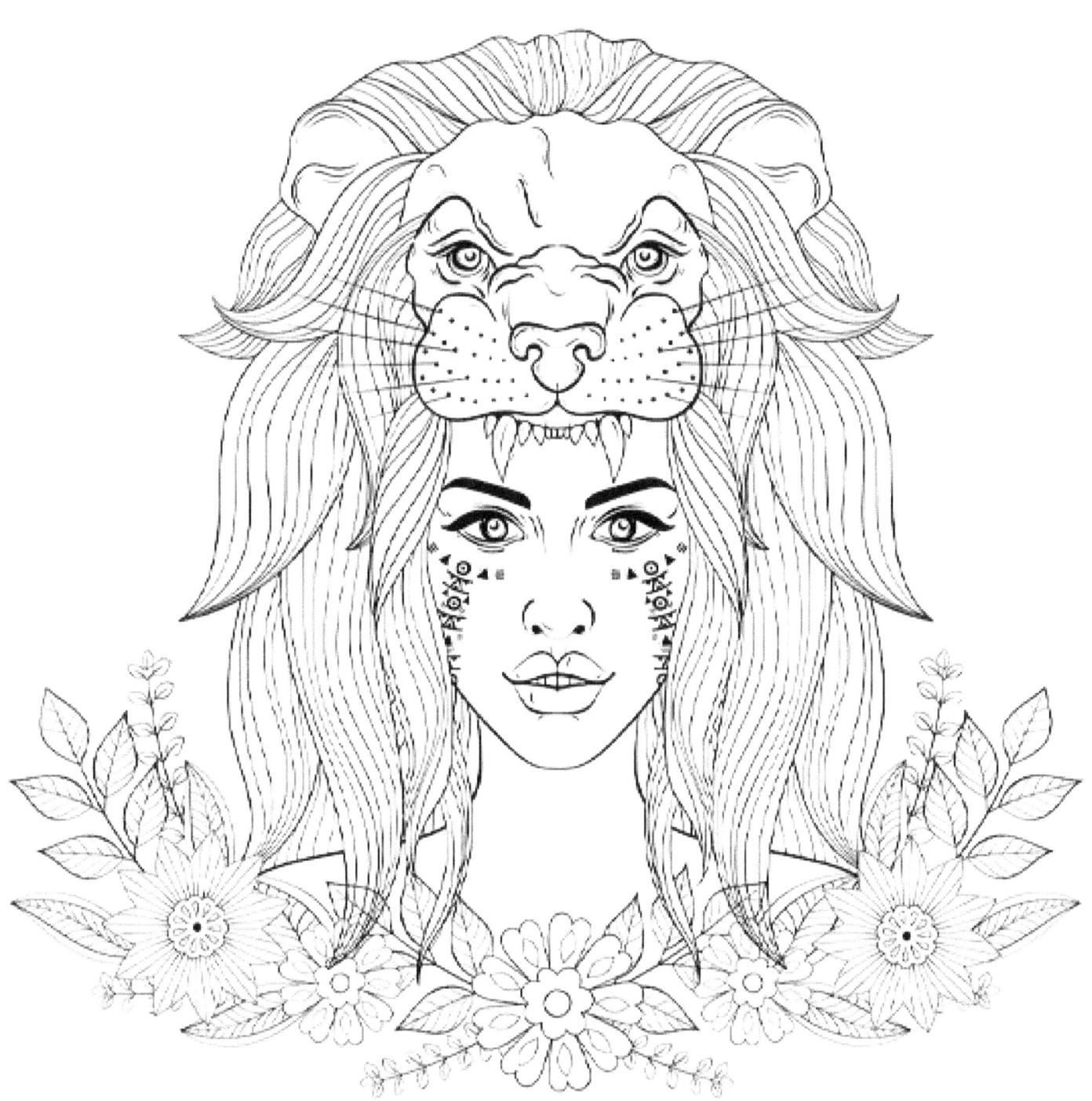

Coloring Test Pages

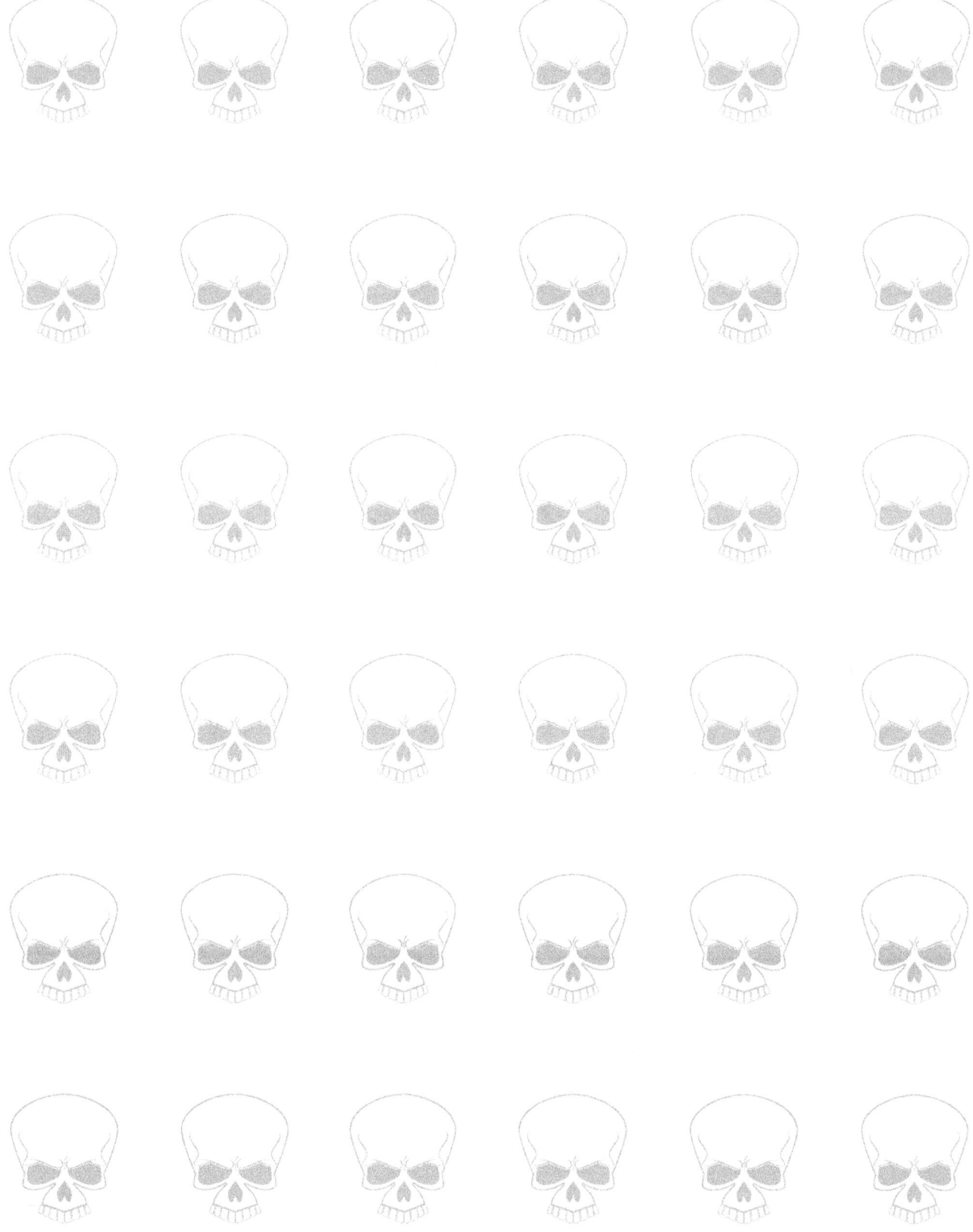

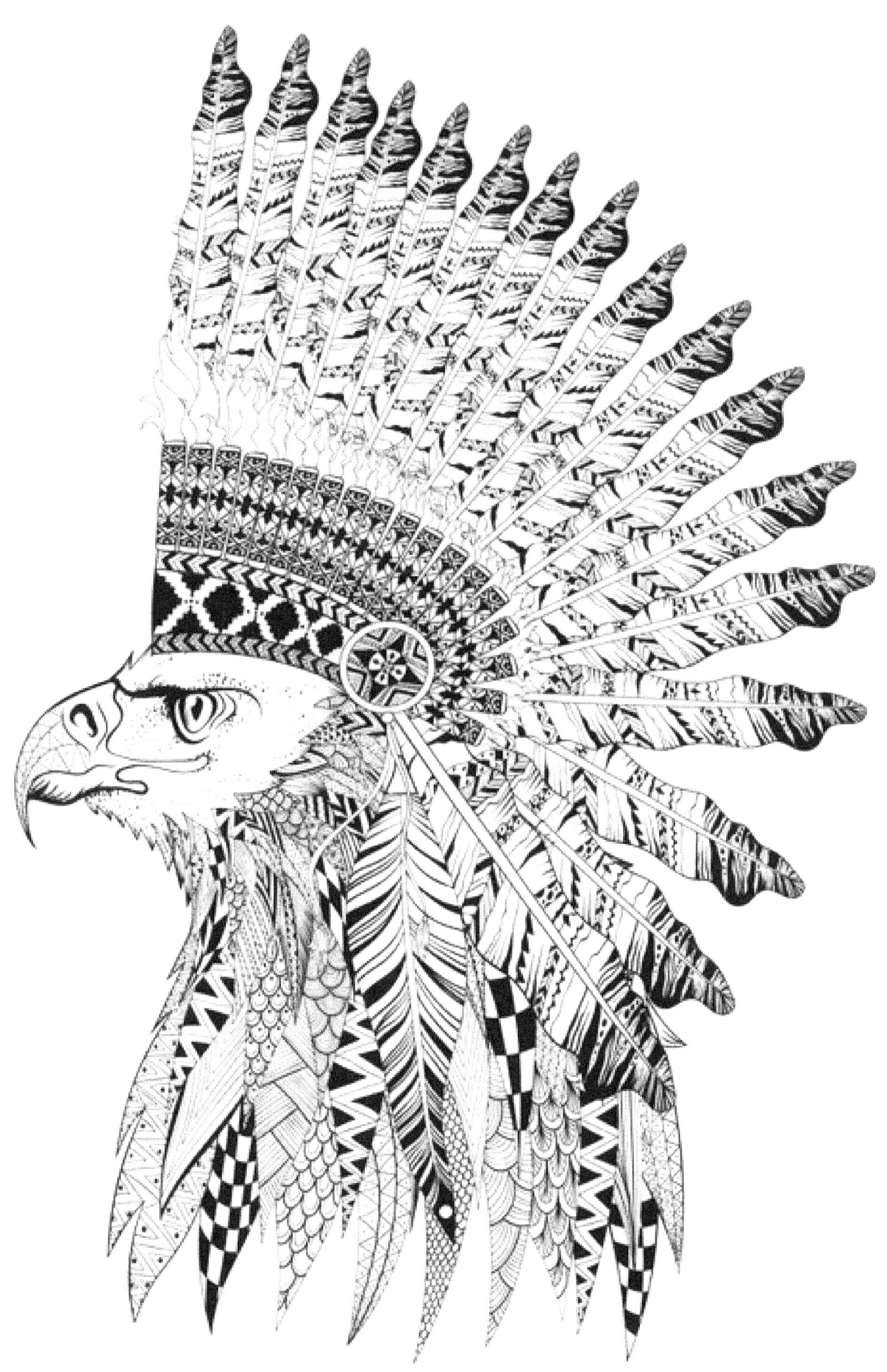

Coloring Test Pages

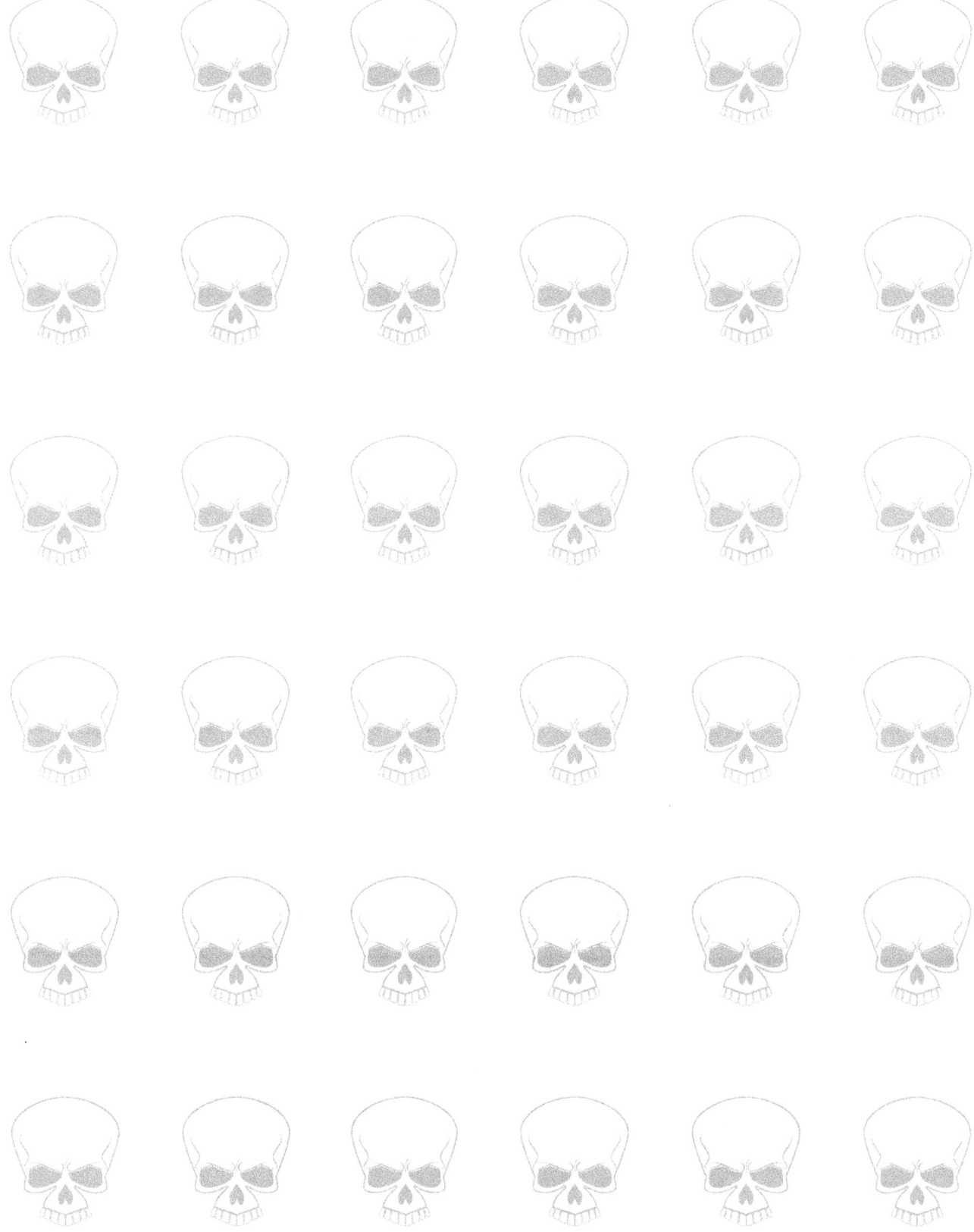

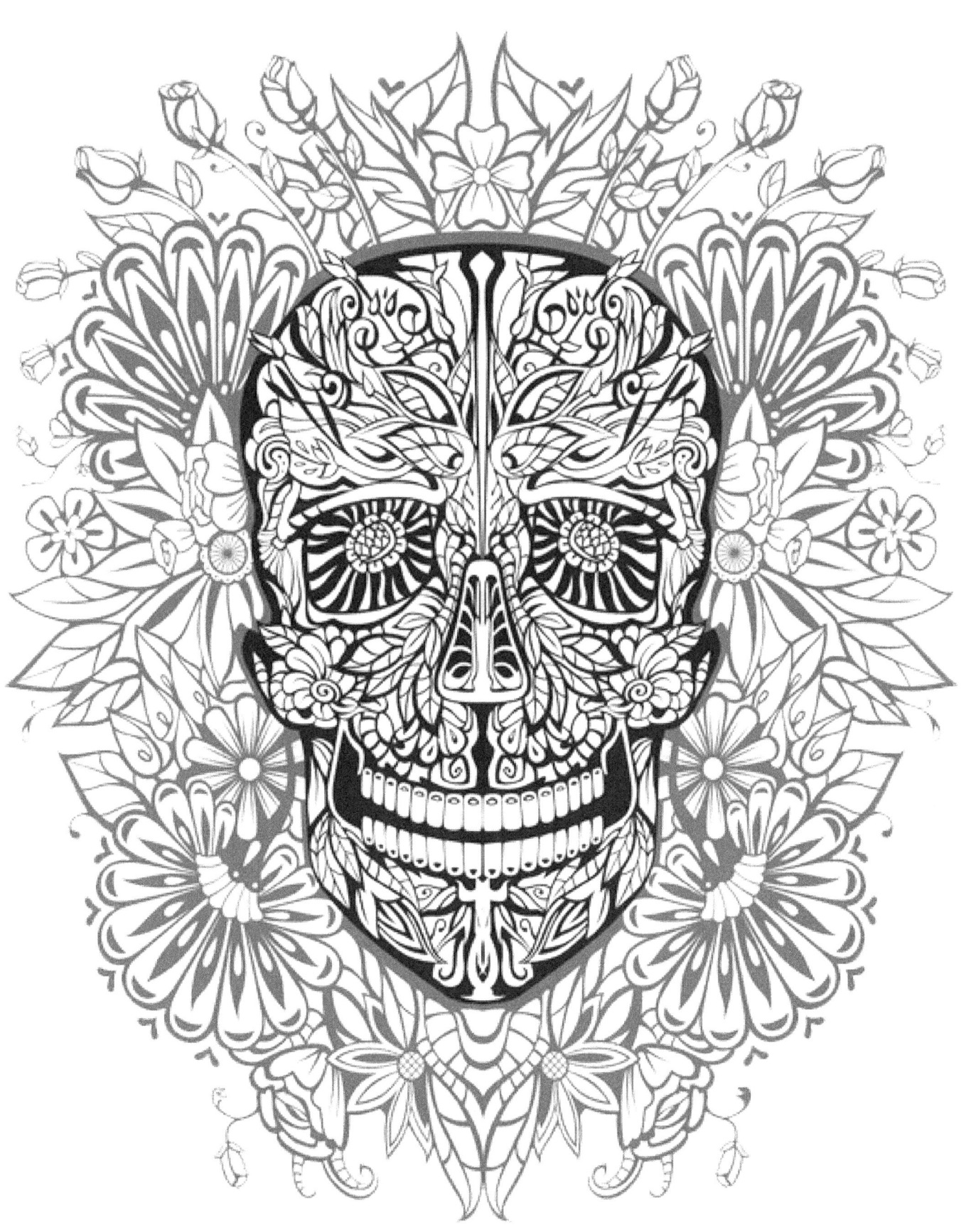

Coloring Test Pages

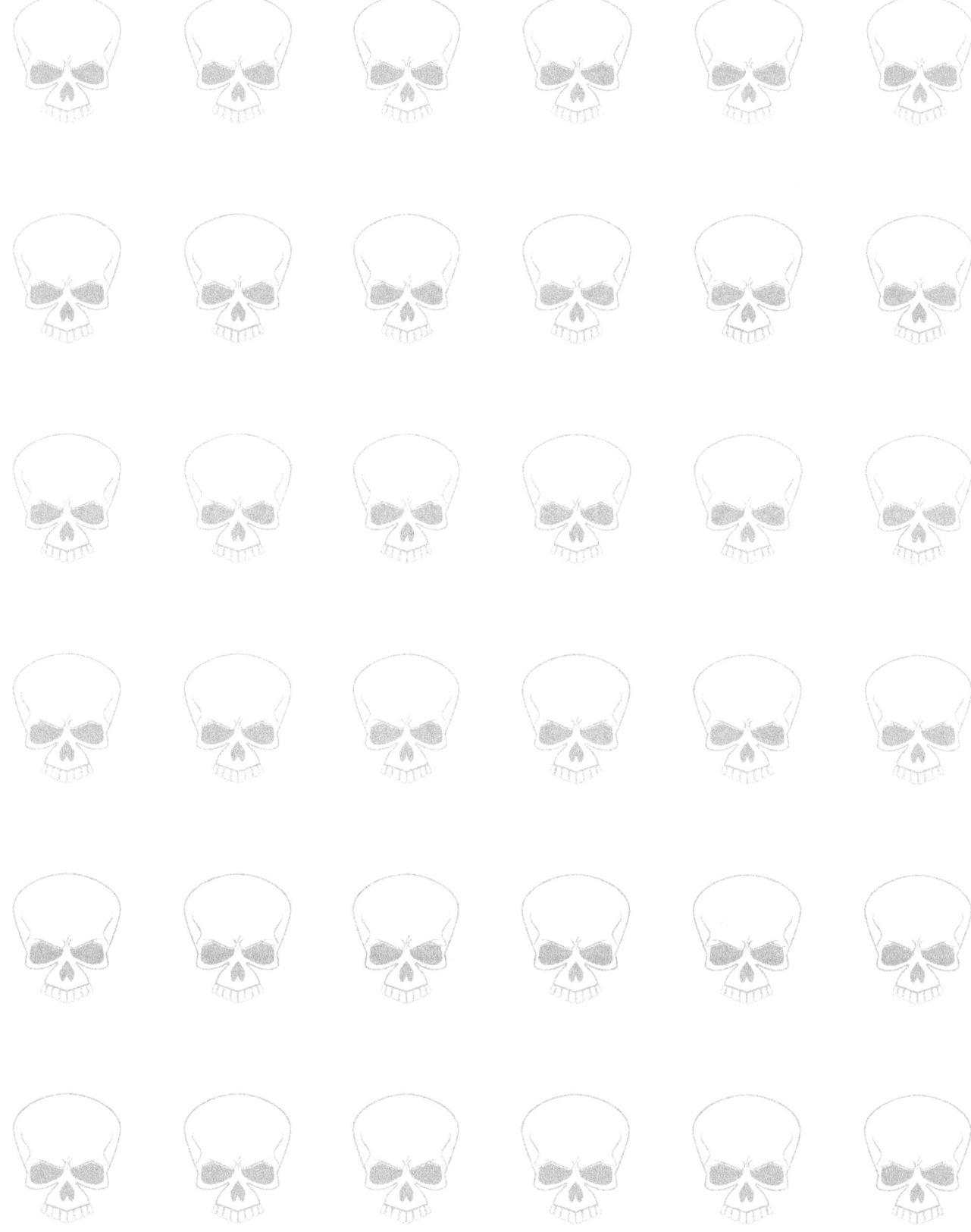

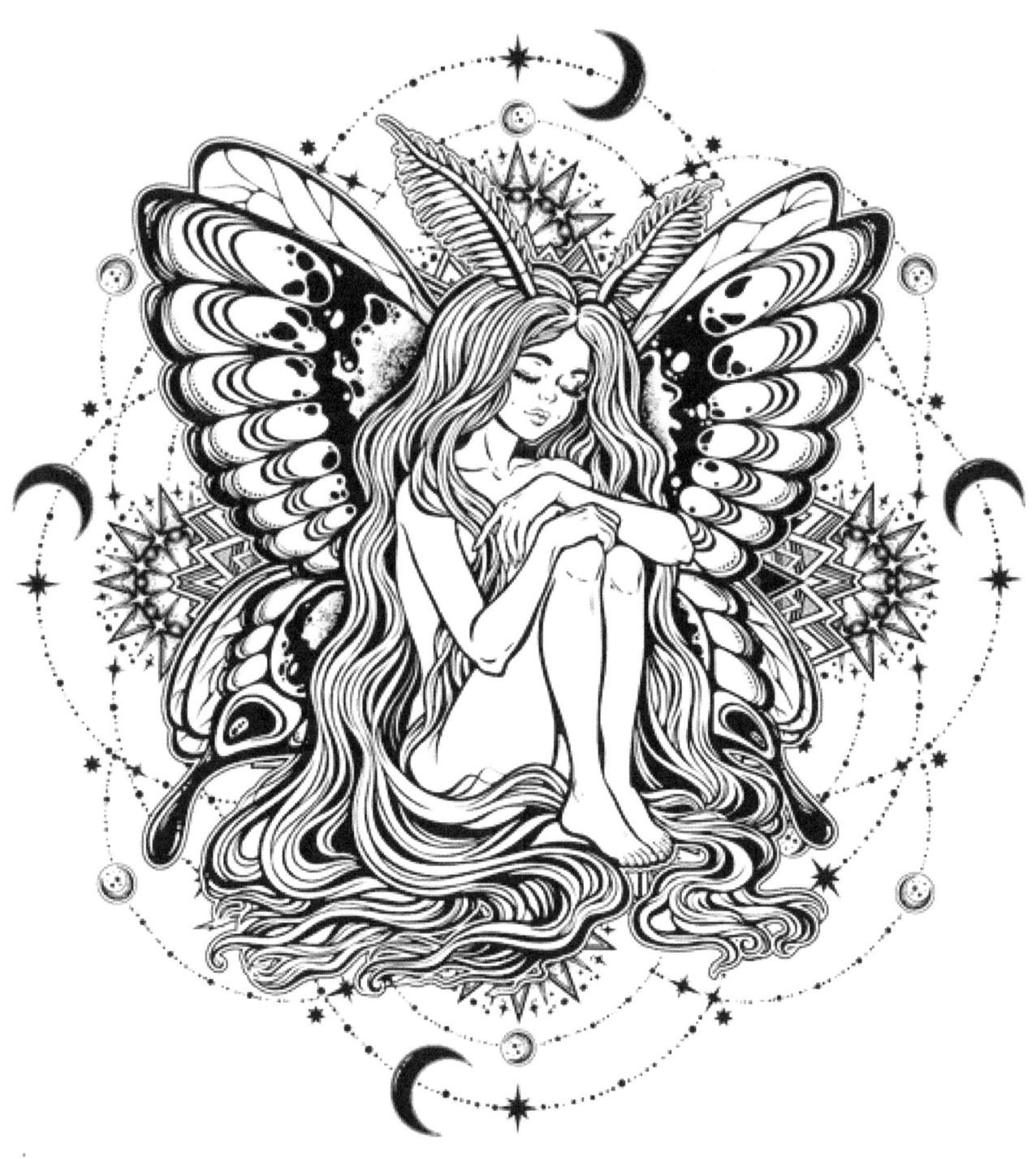

Coloring Test Pages

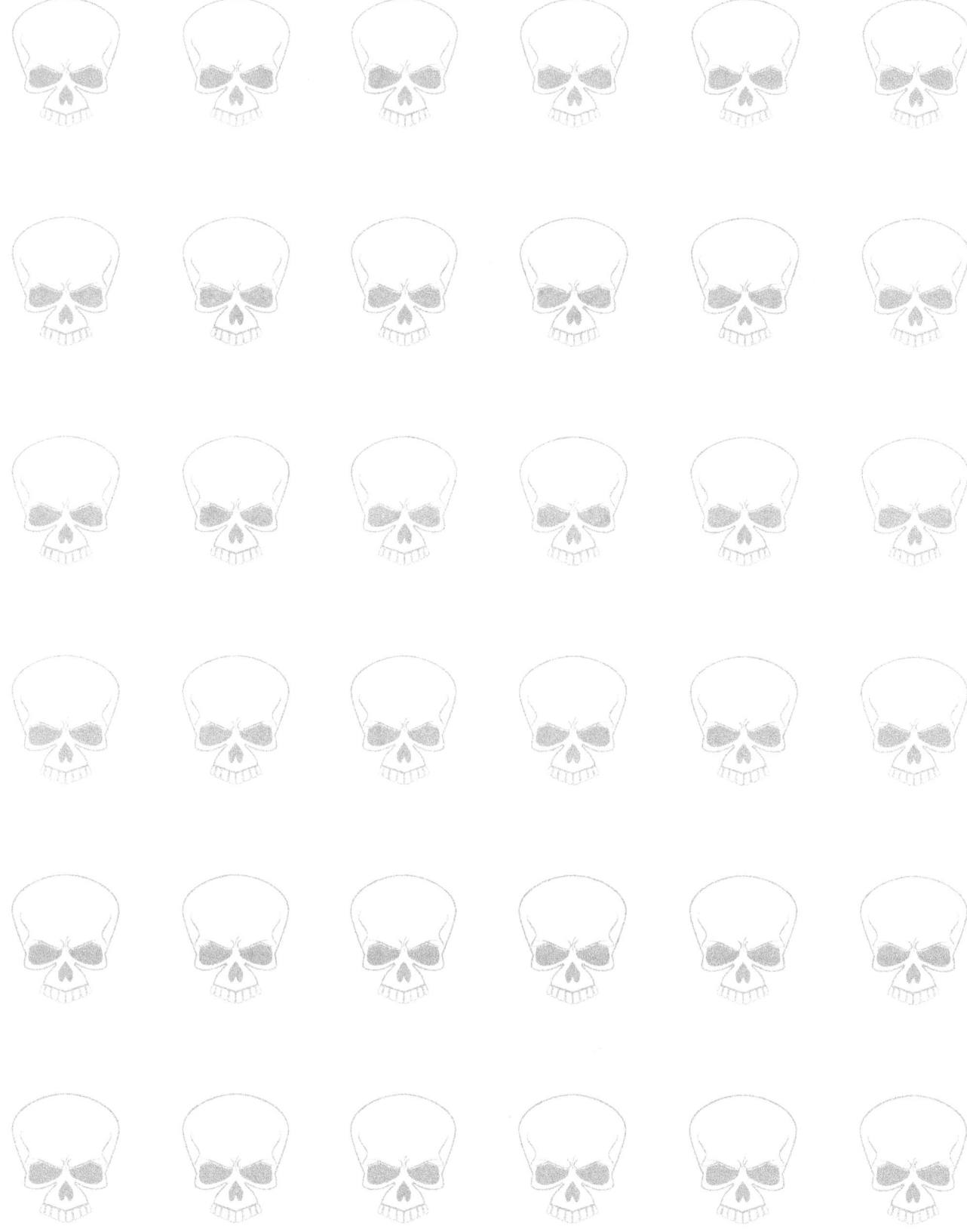

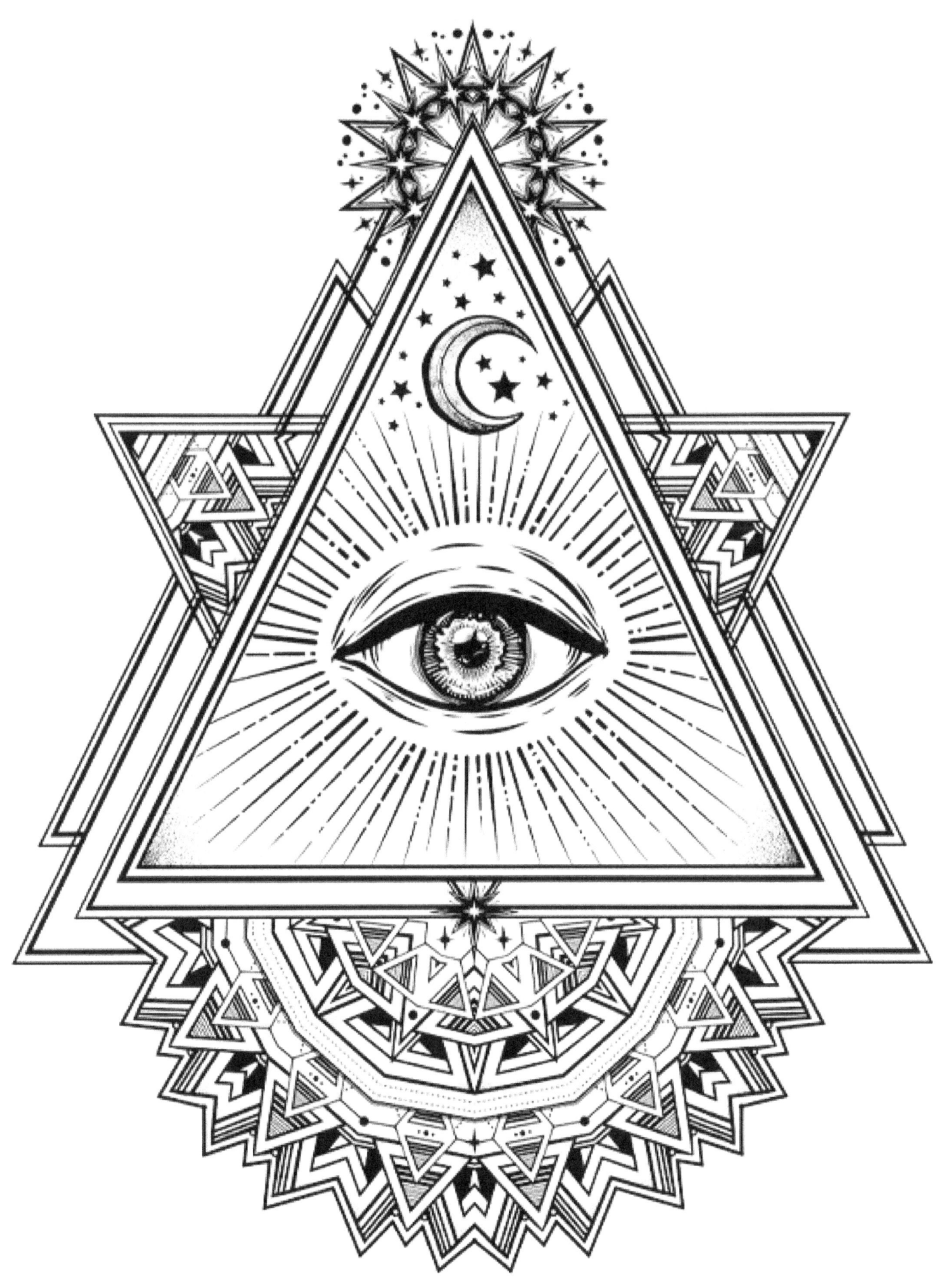

Coloring Test Pages

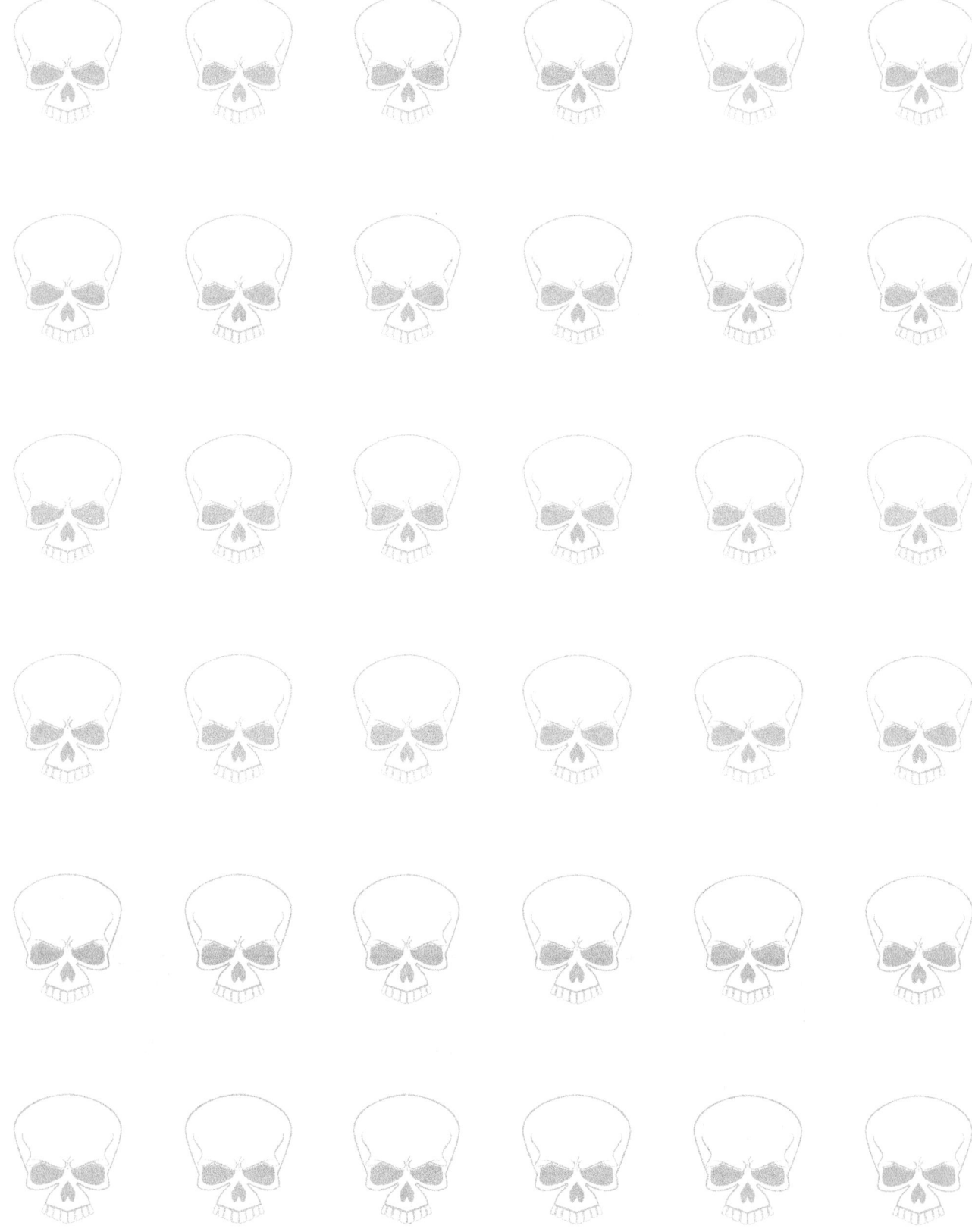

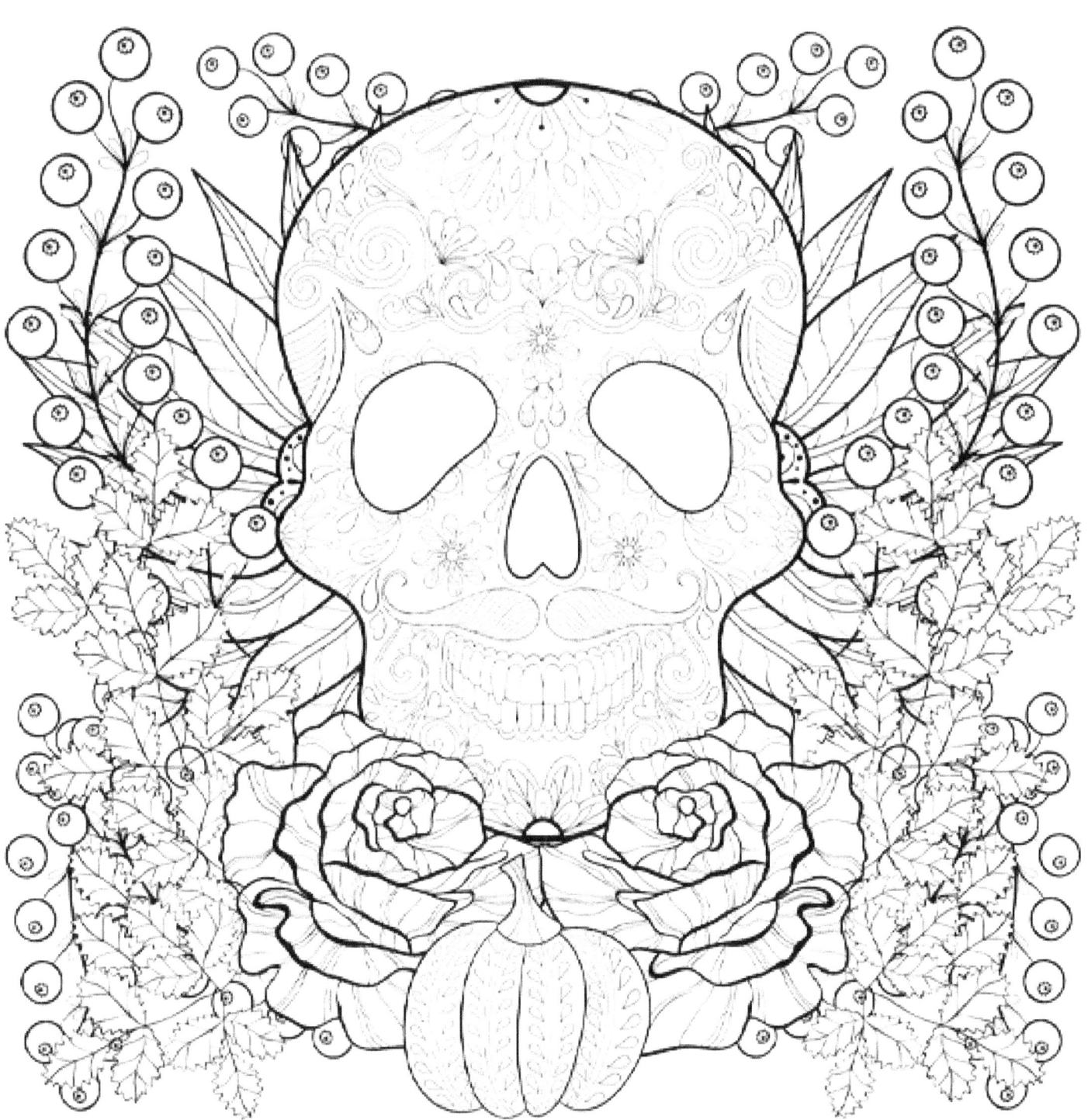

Coloring Test Pages

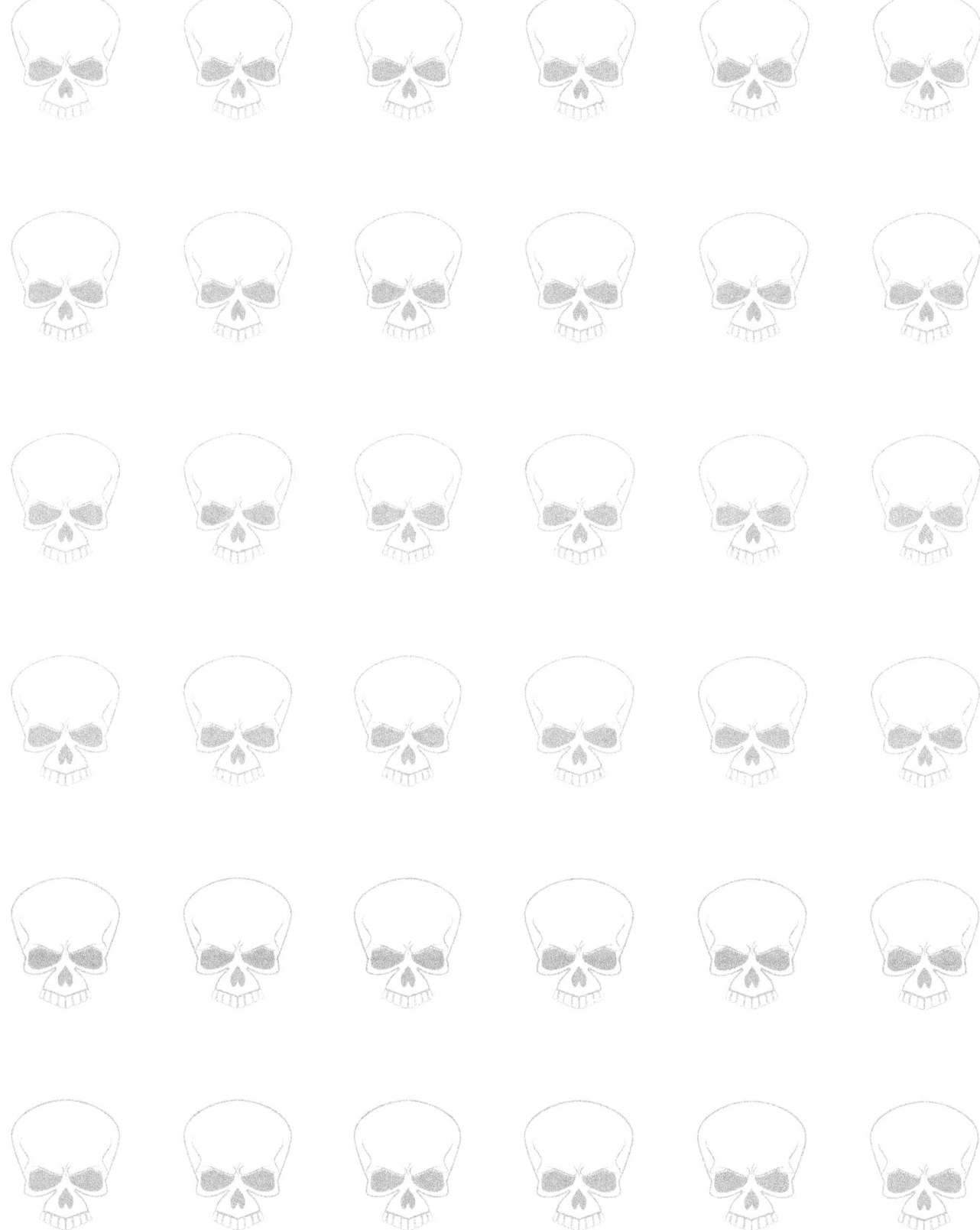

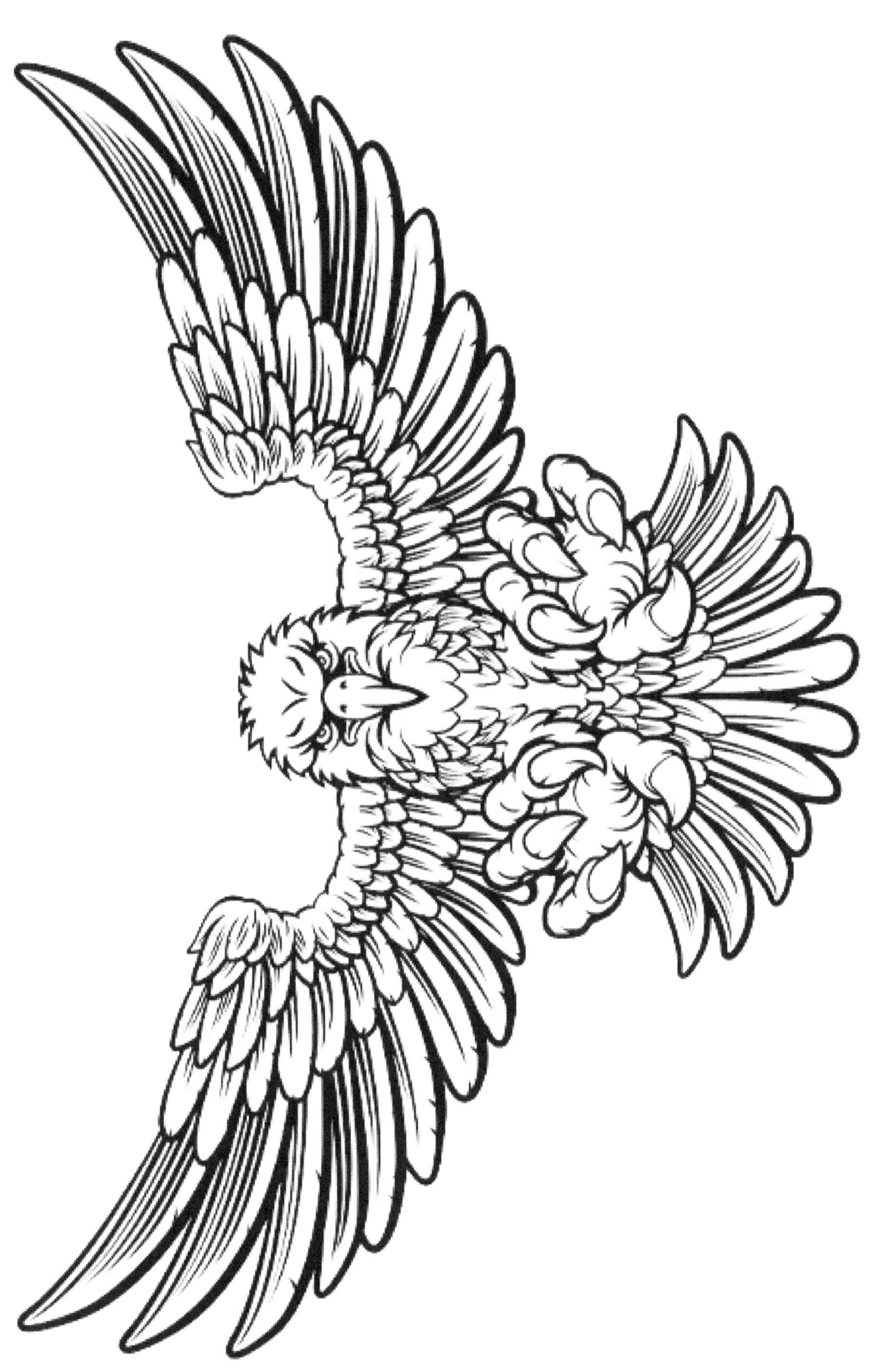

Coloring Test Pages

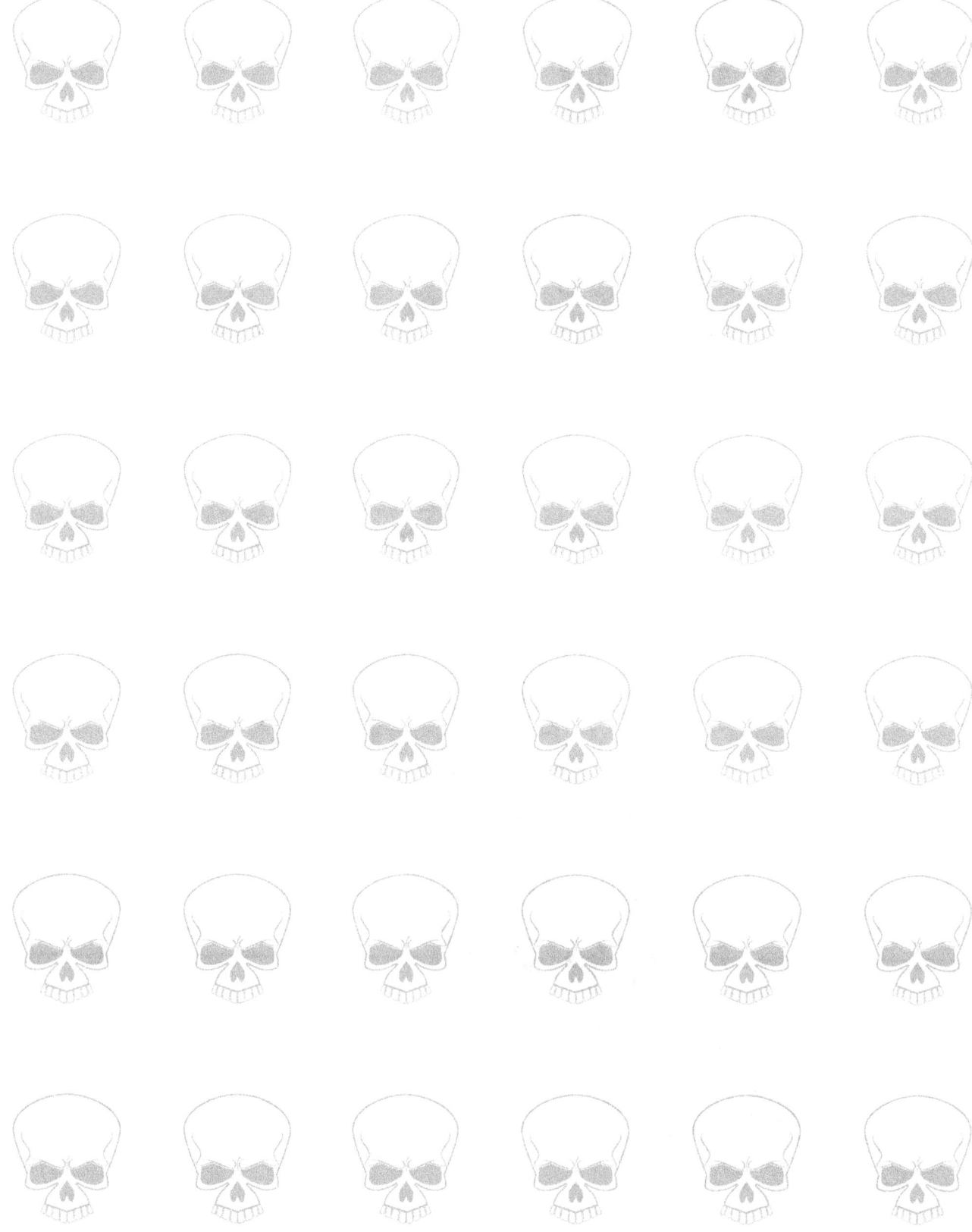

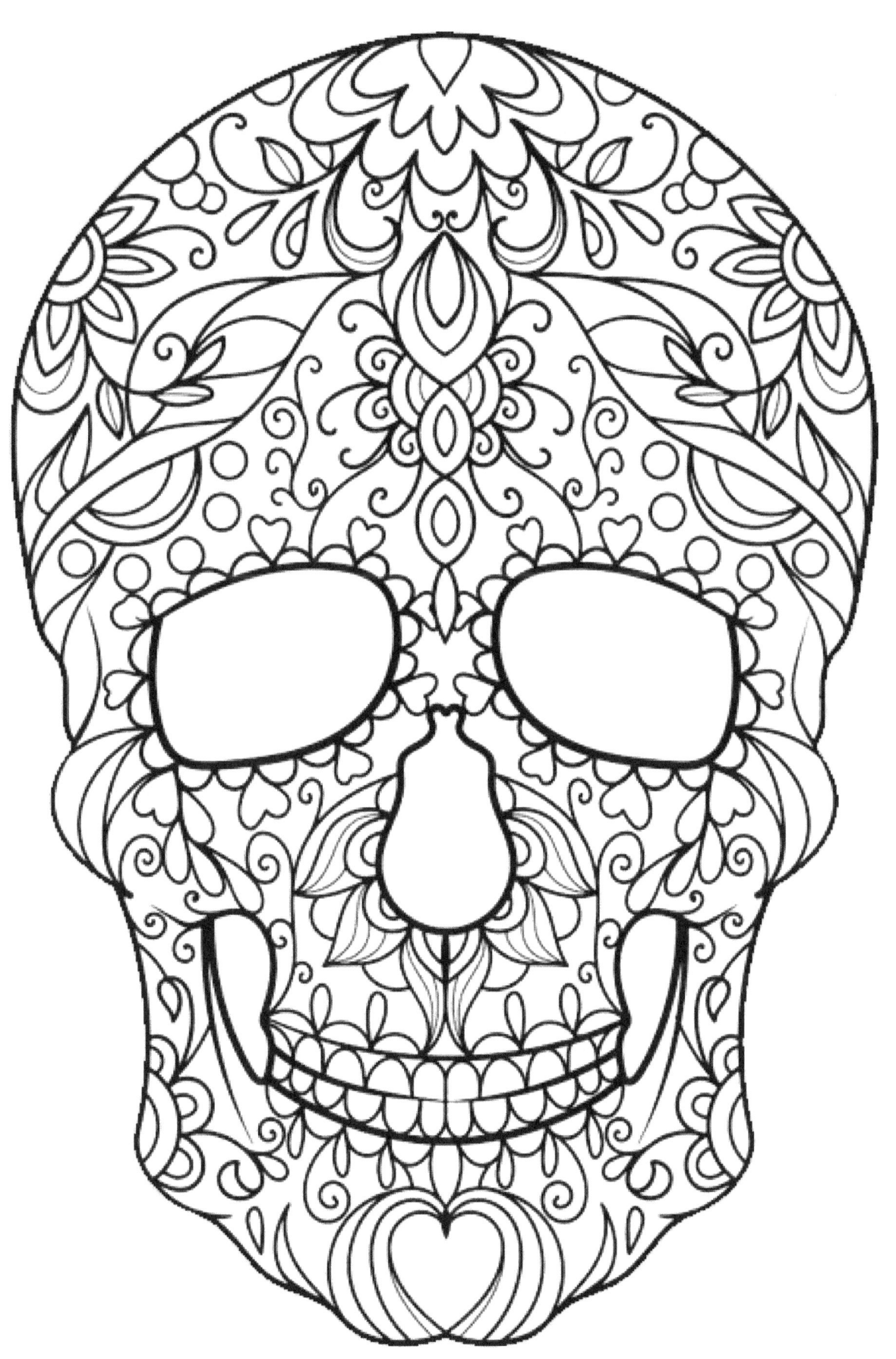

Coloring Test Pages

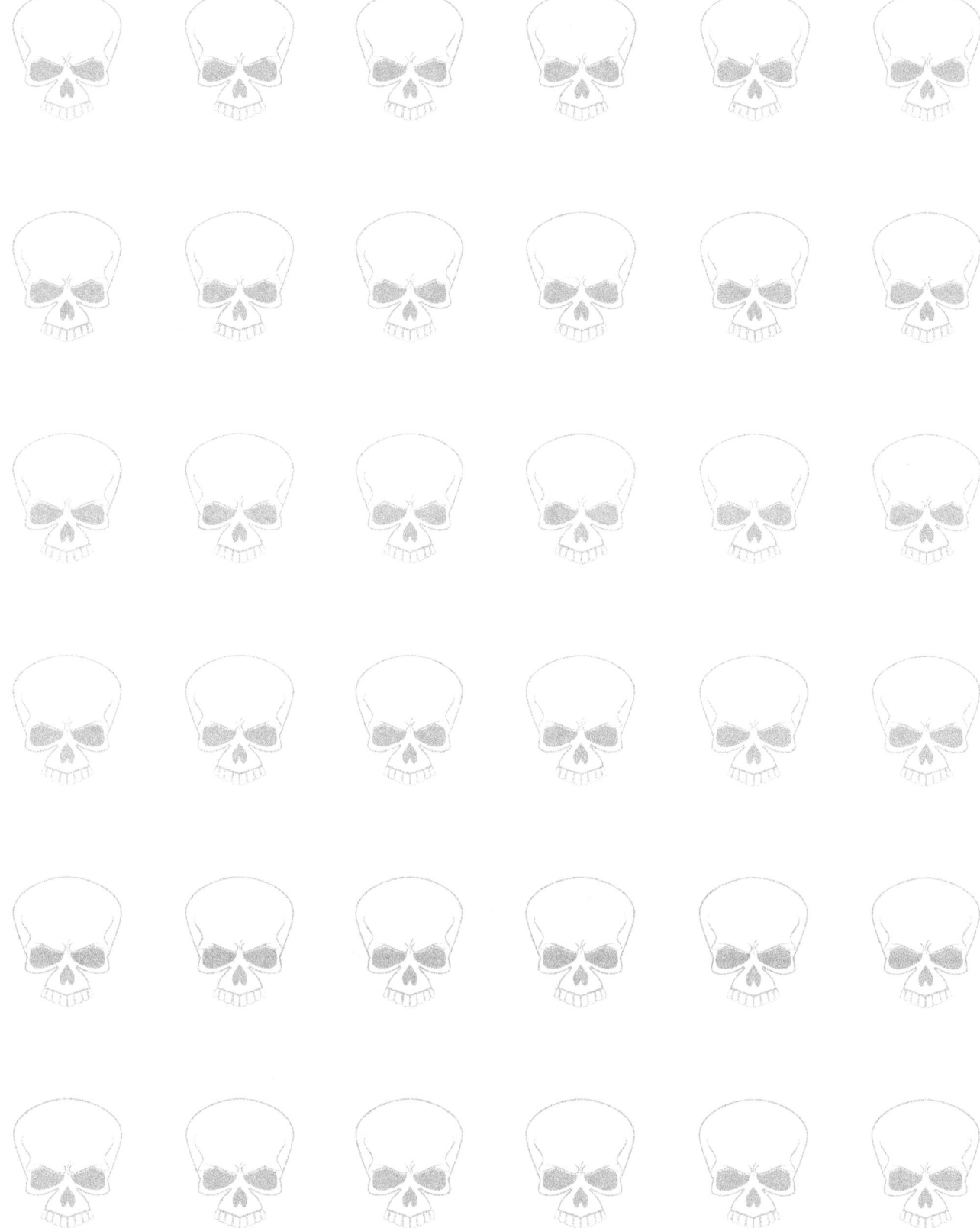

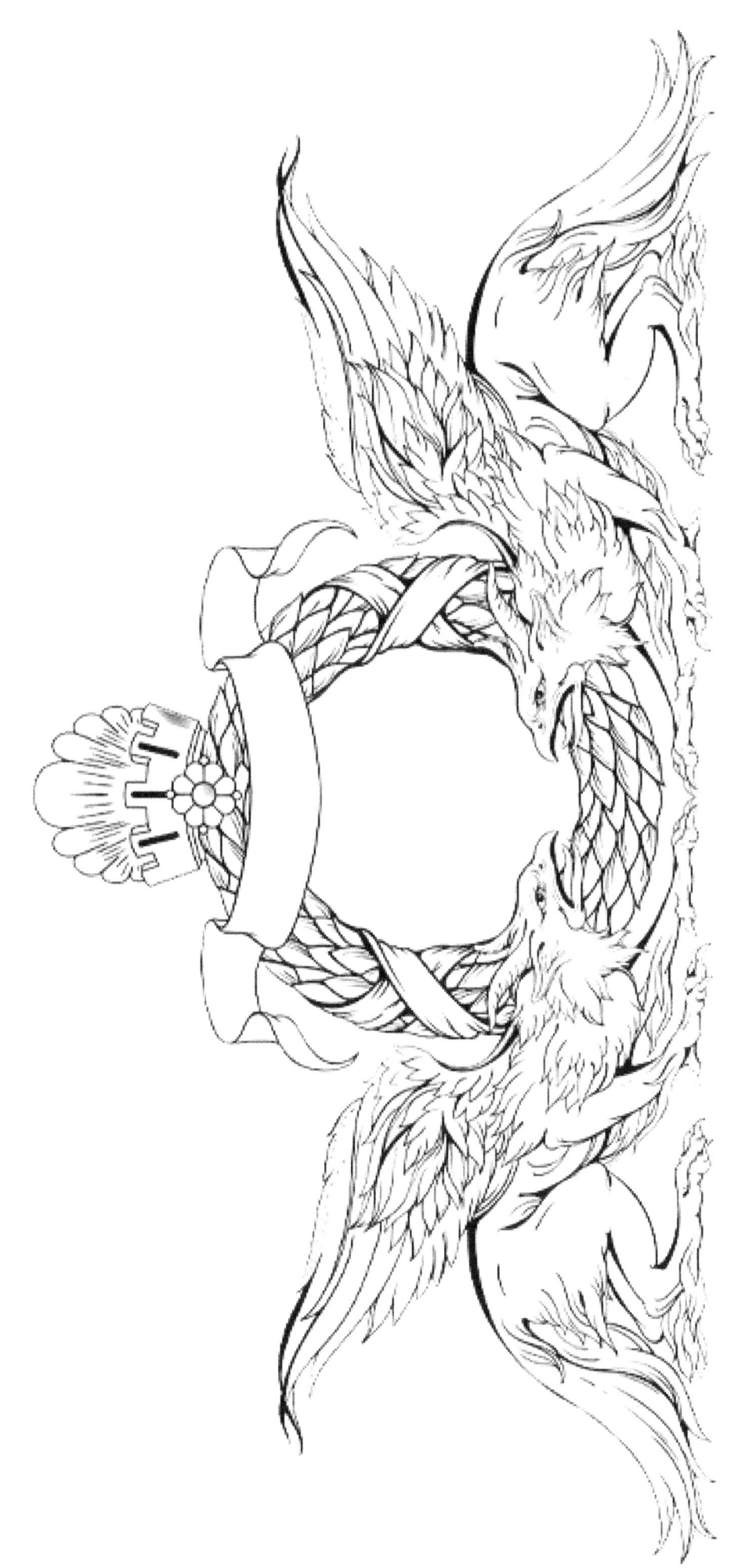

Coloring Test Pages

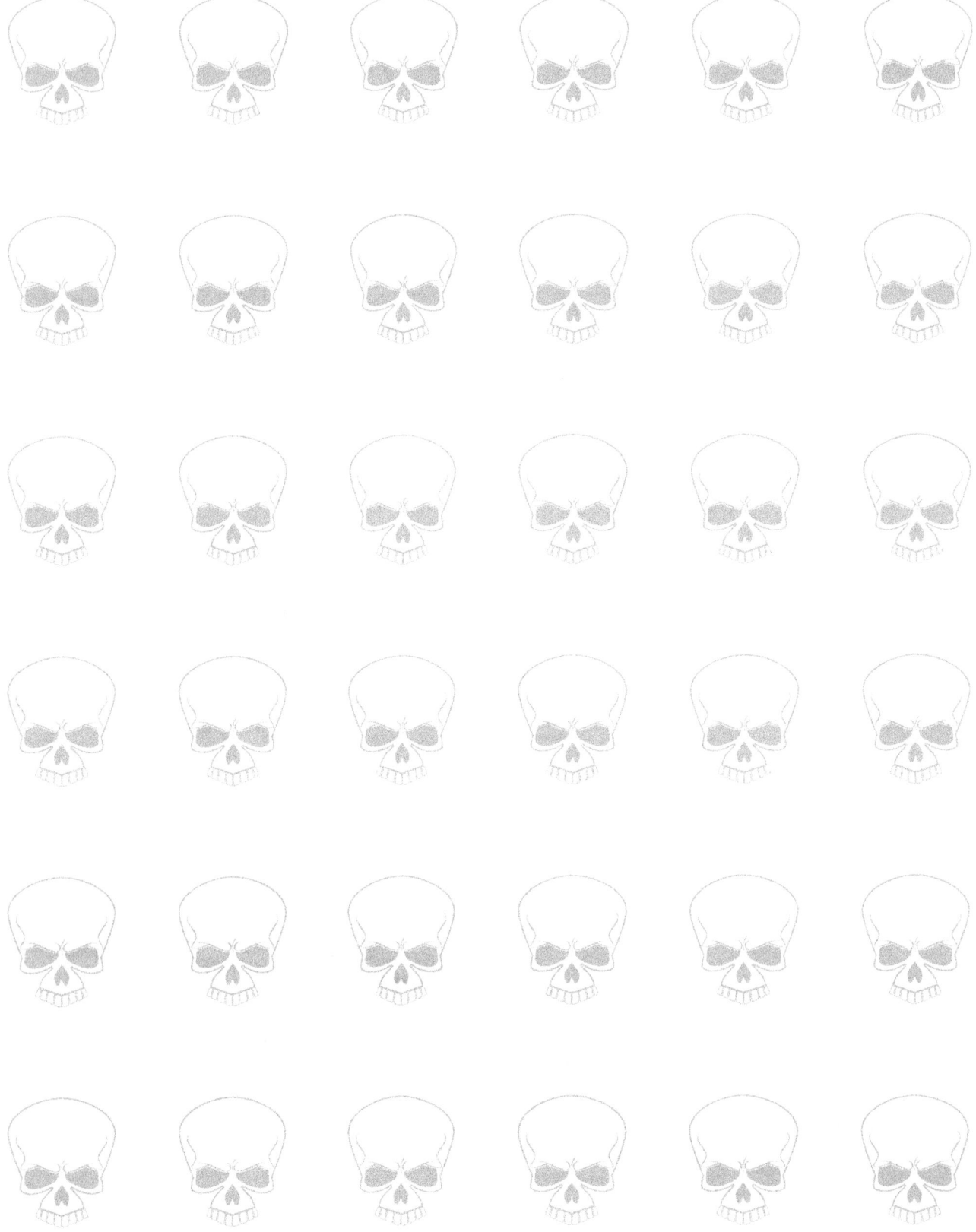

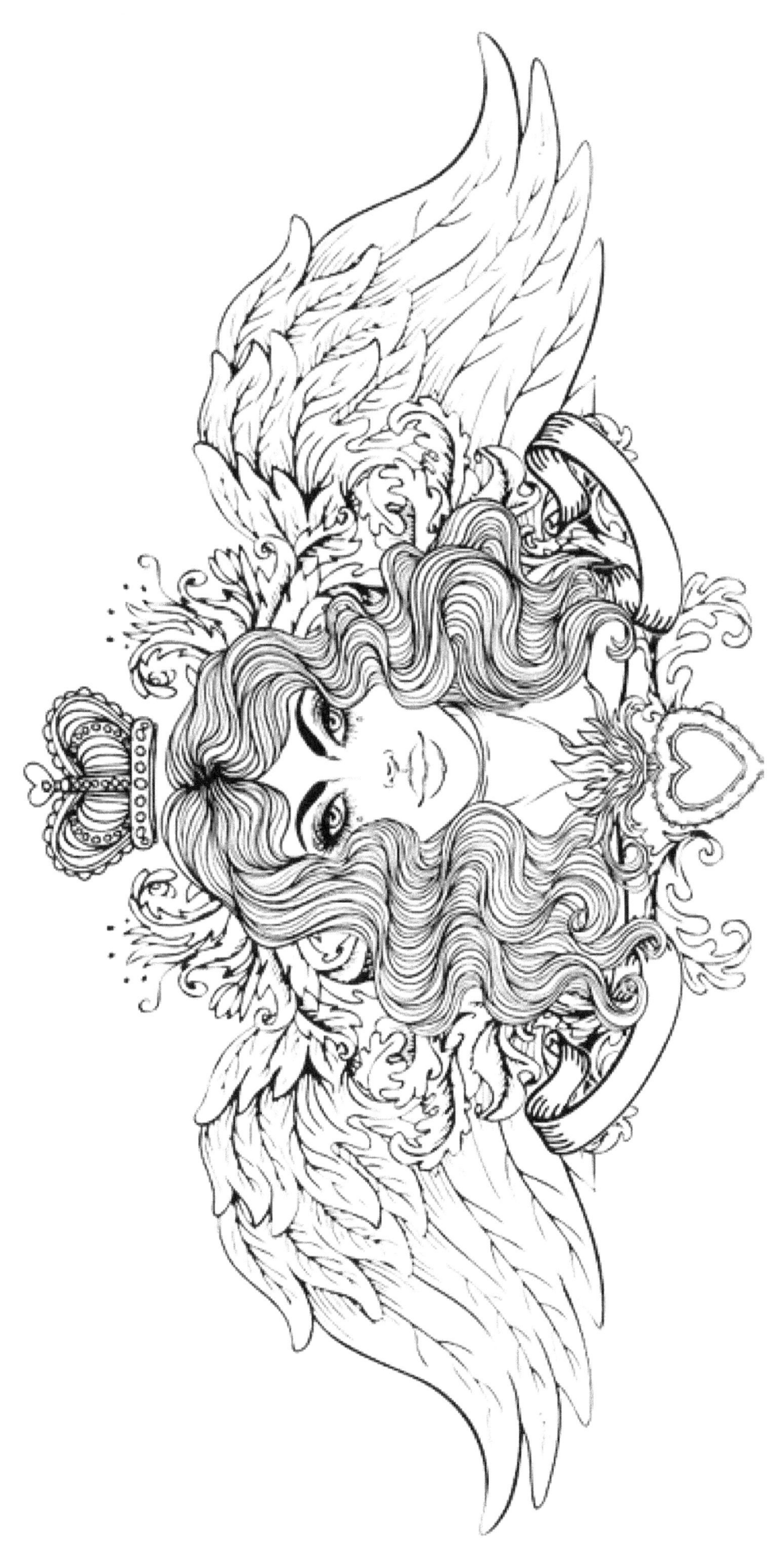

Coloring Test Pages

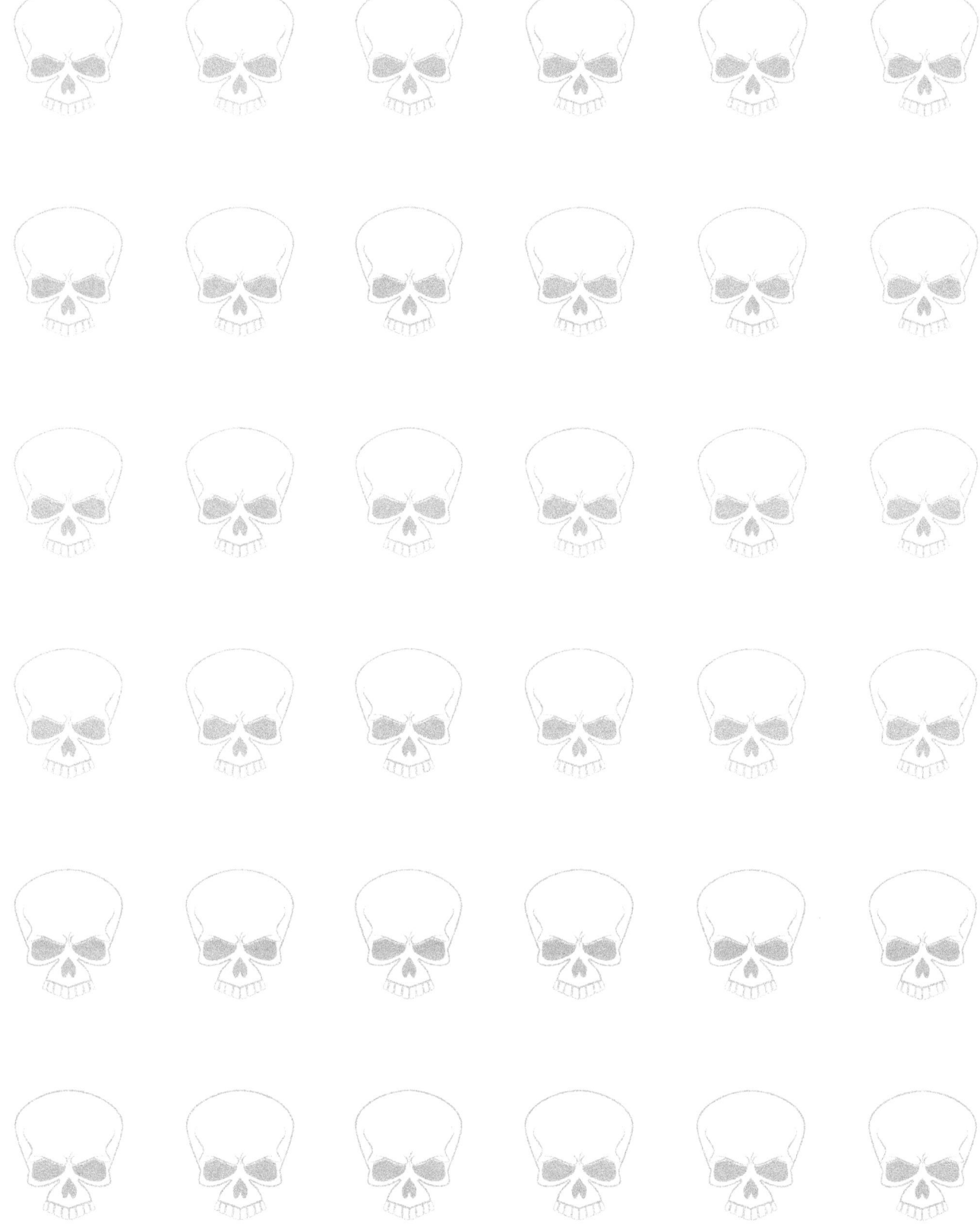

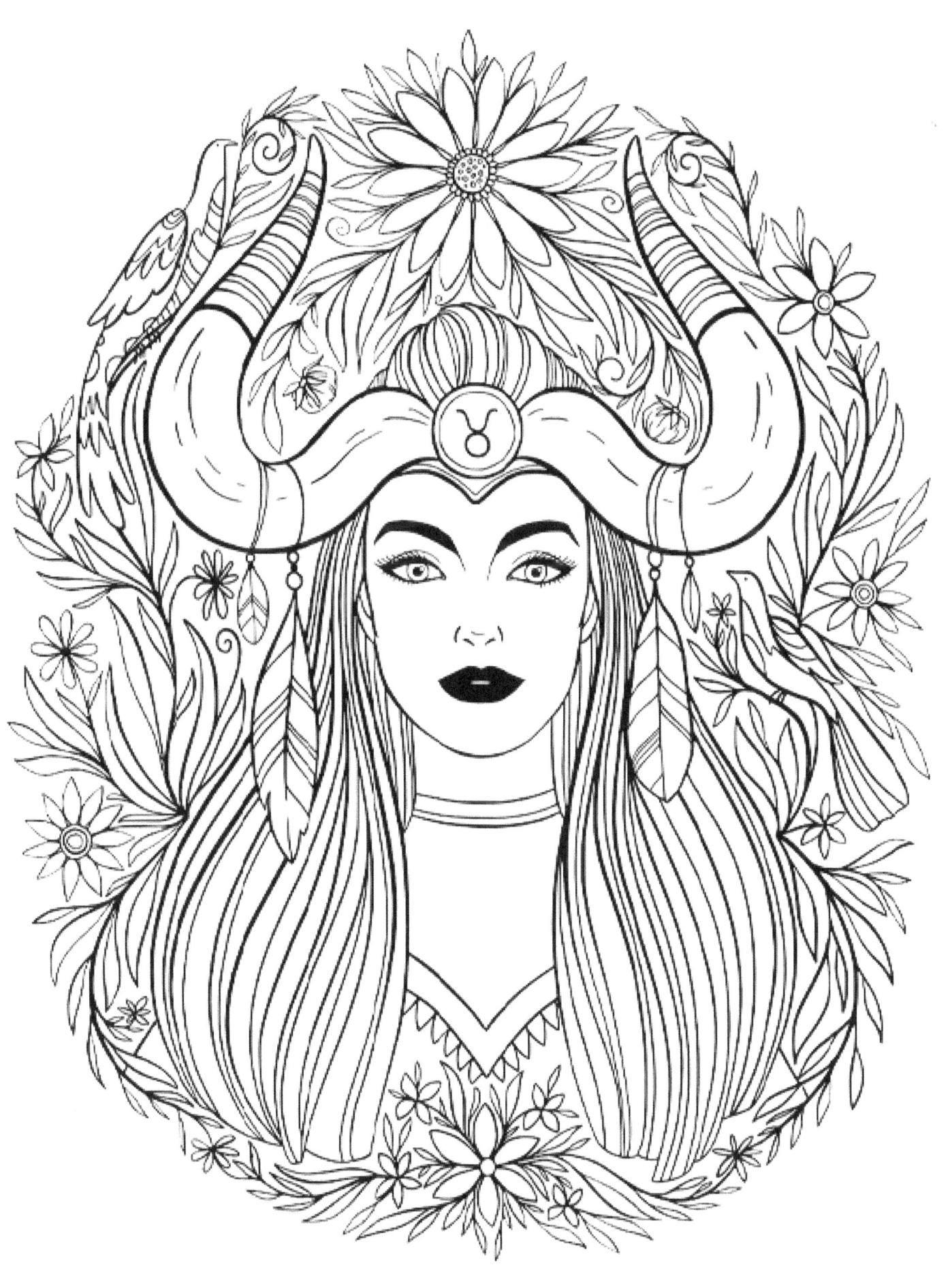

Coloring Test Pages

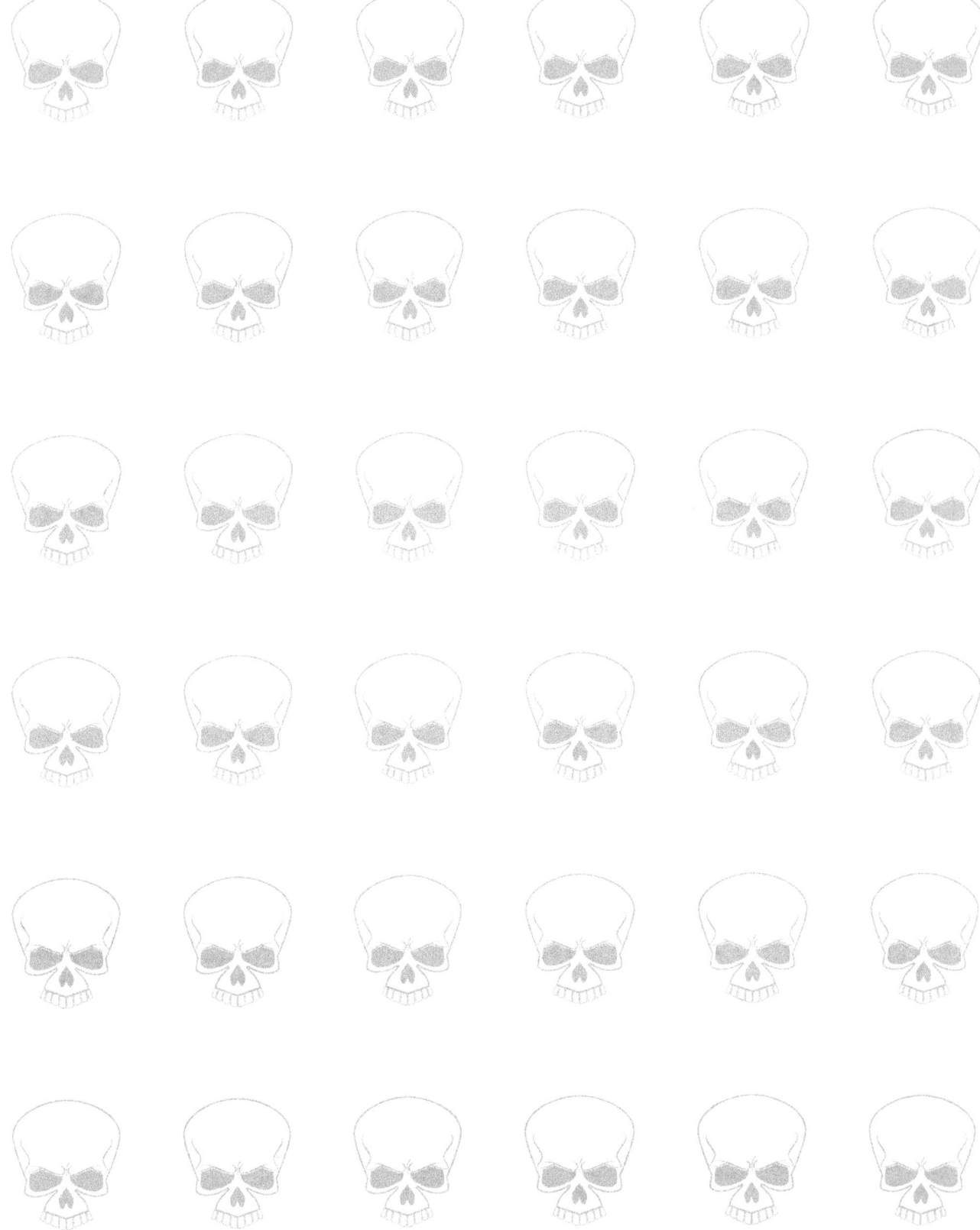

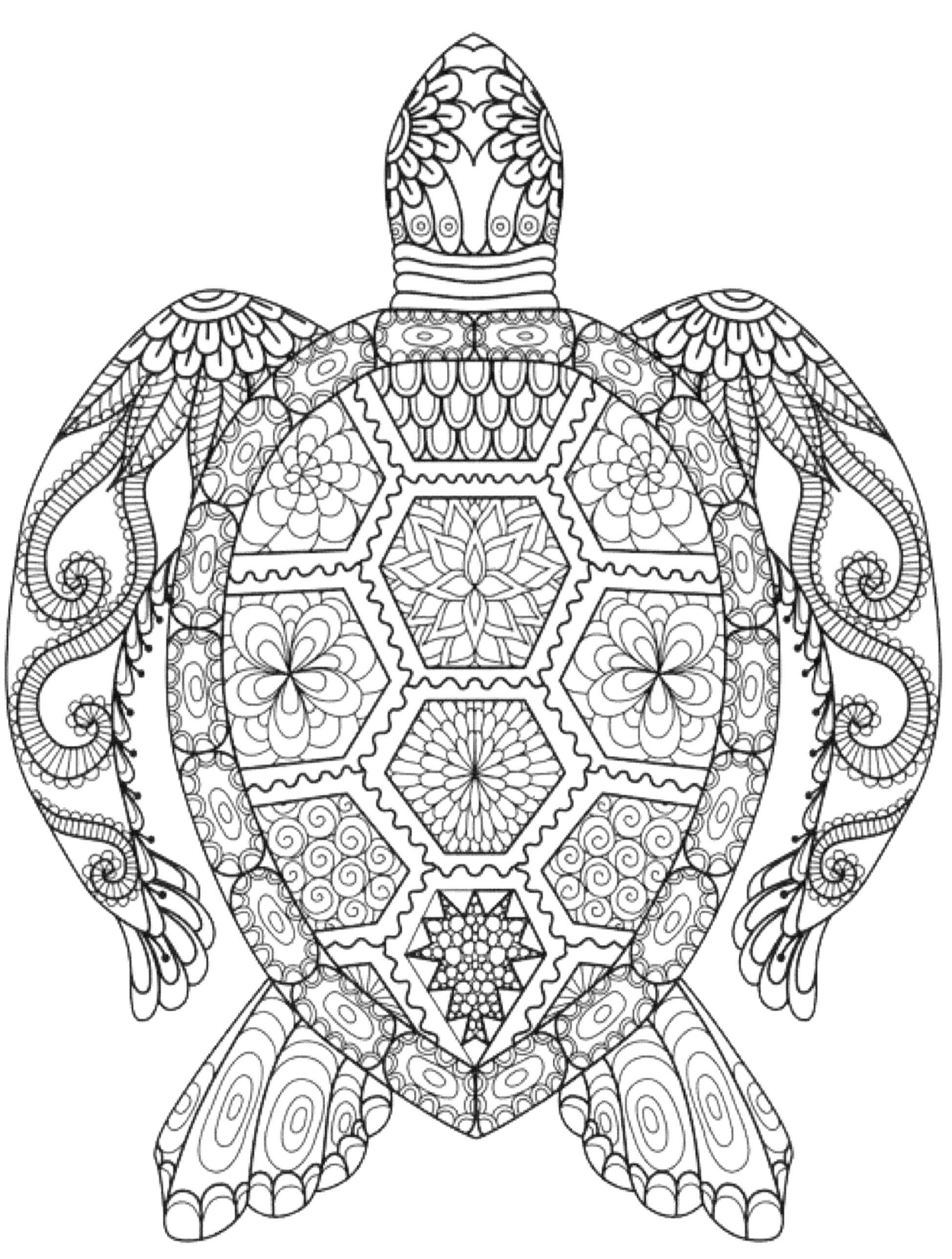

Coloring Test Pages

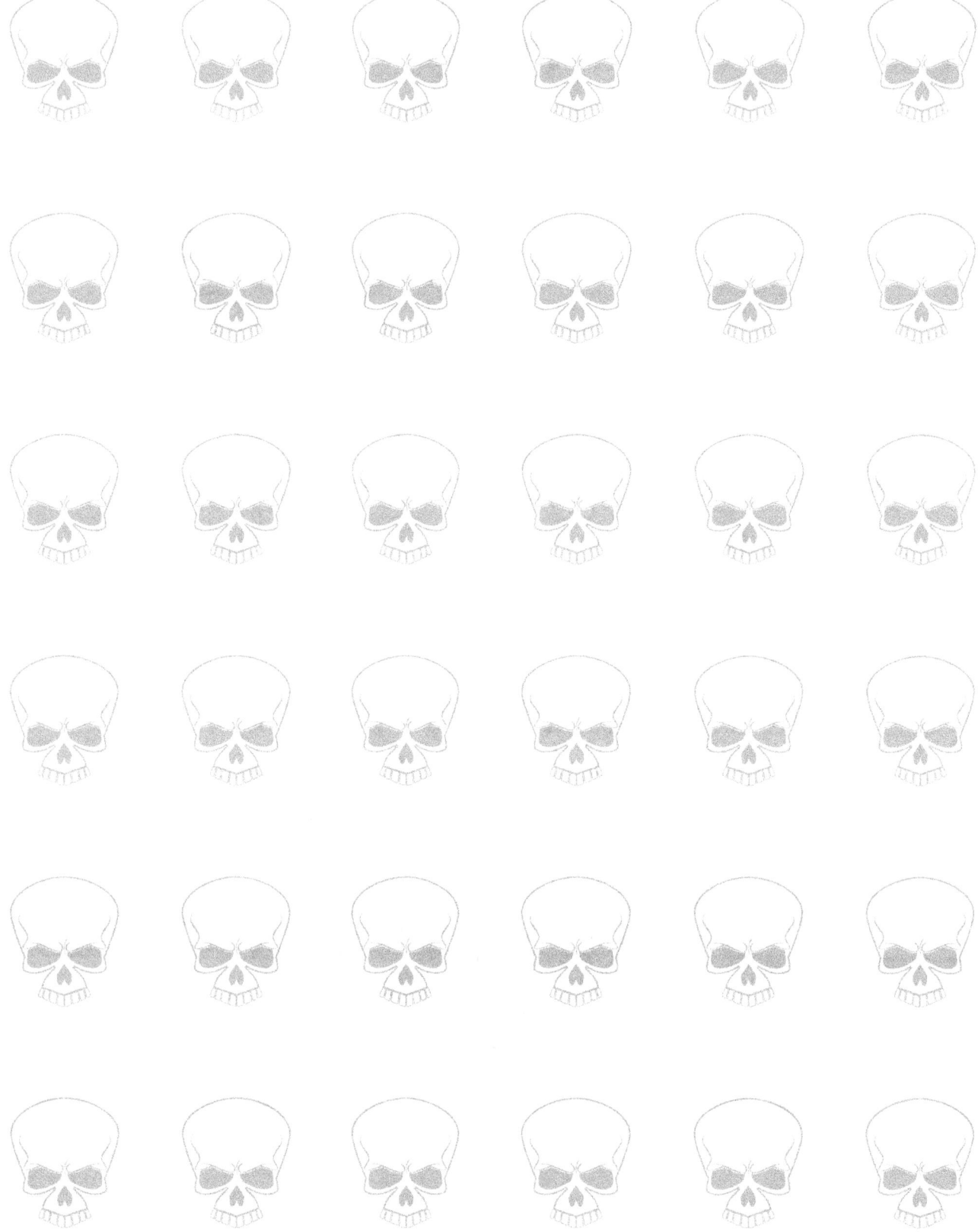

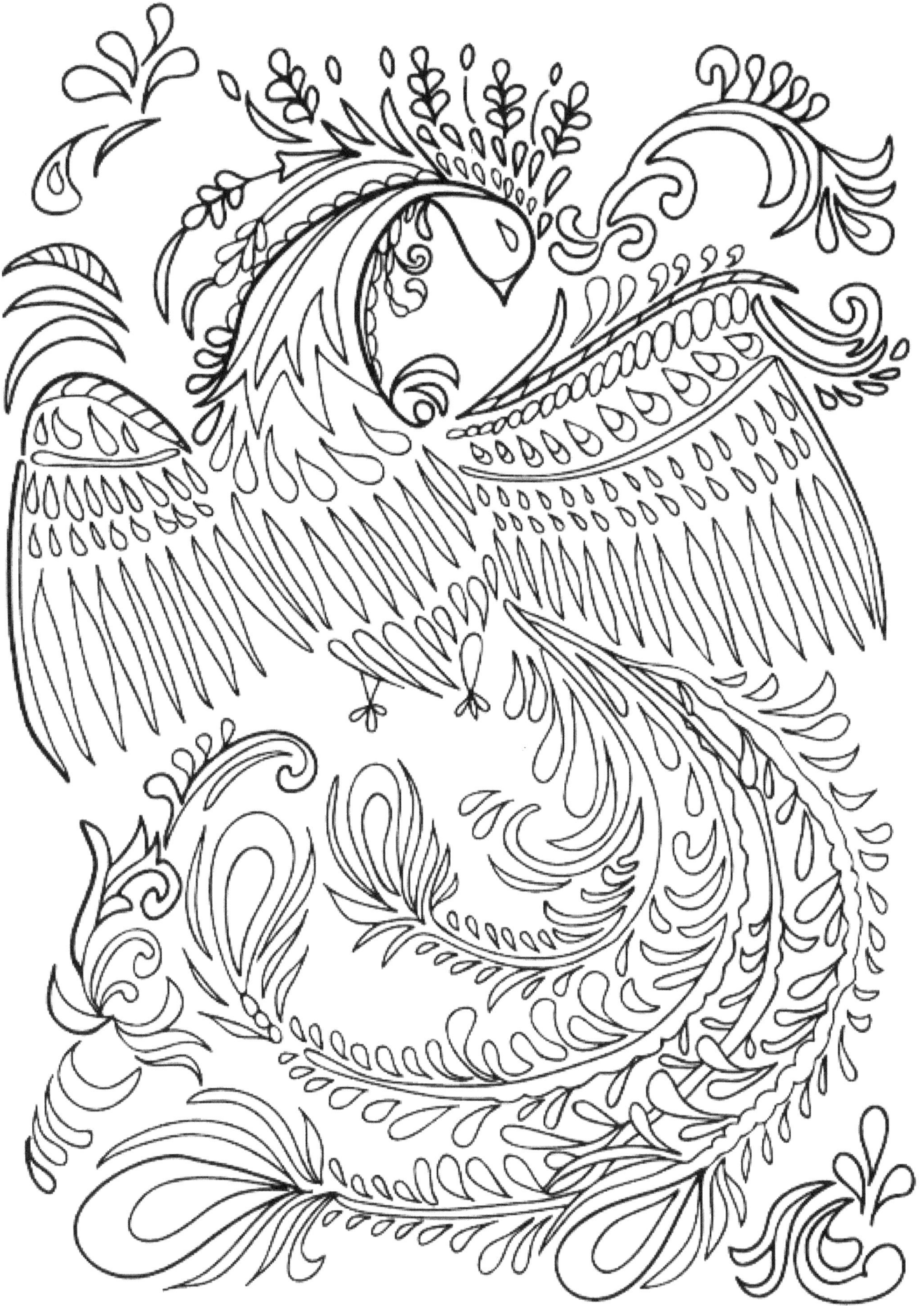

Coloring Test Pages

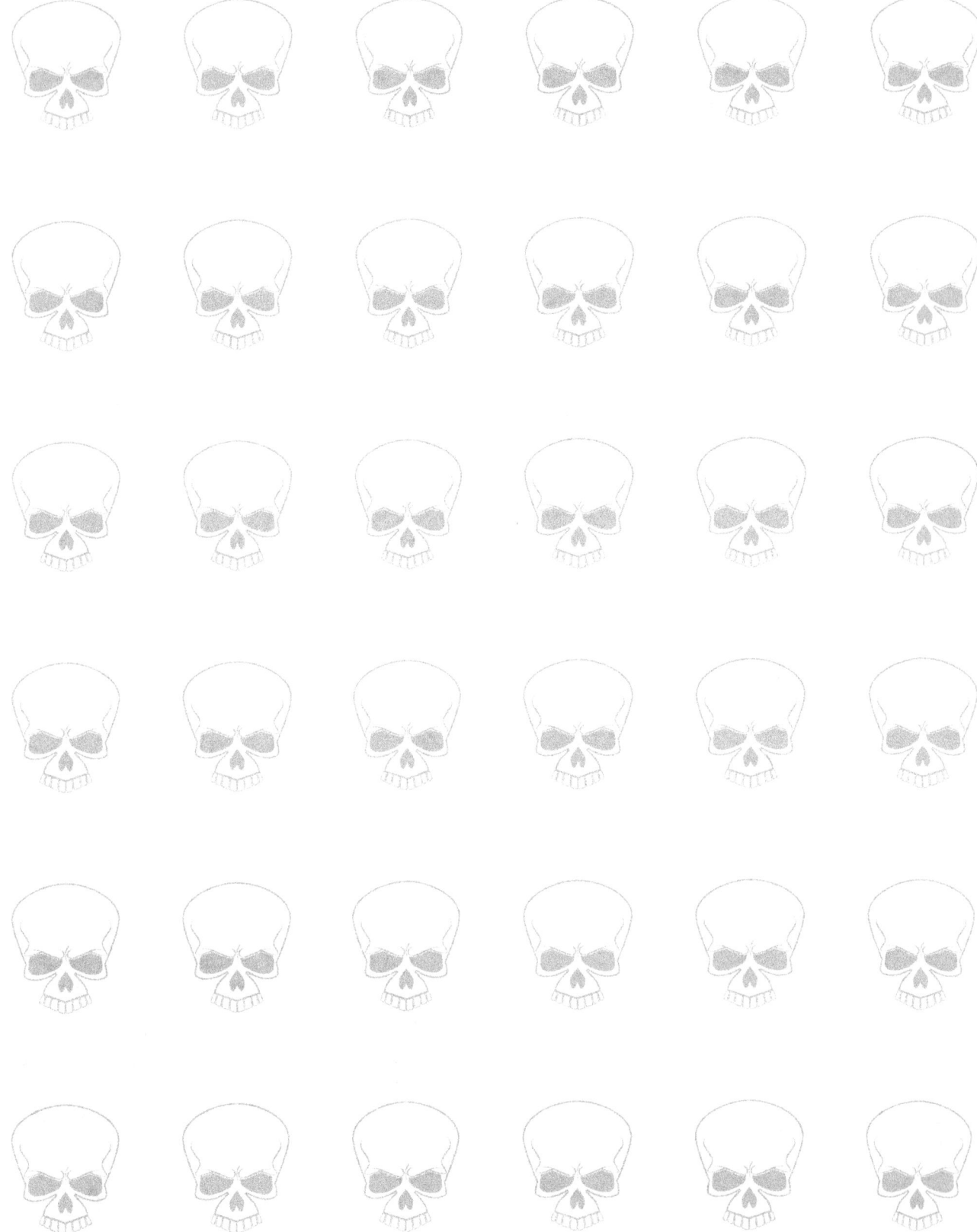

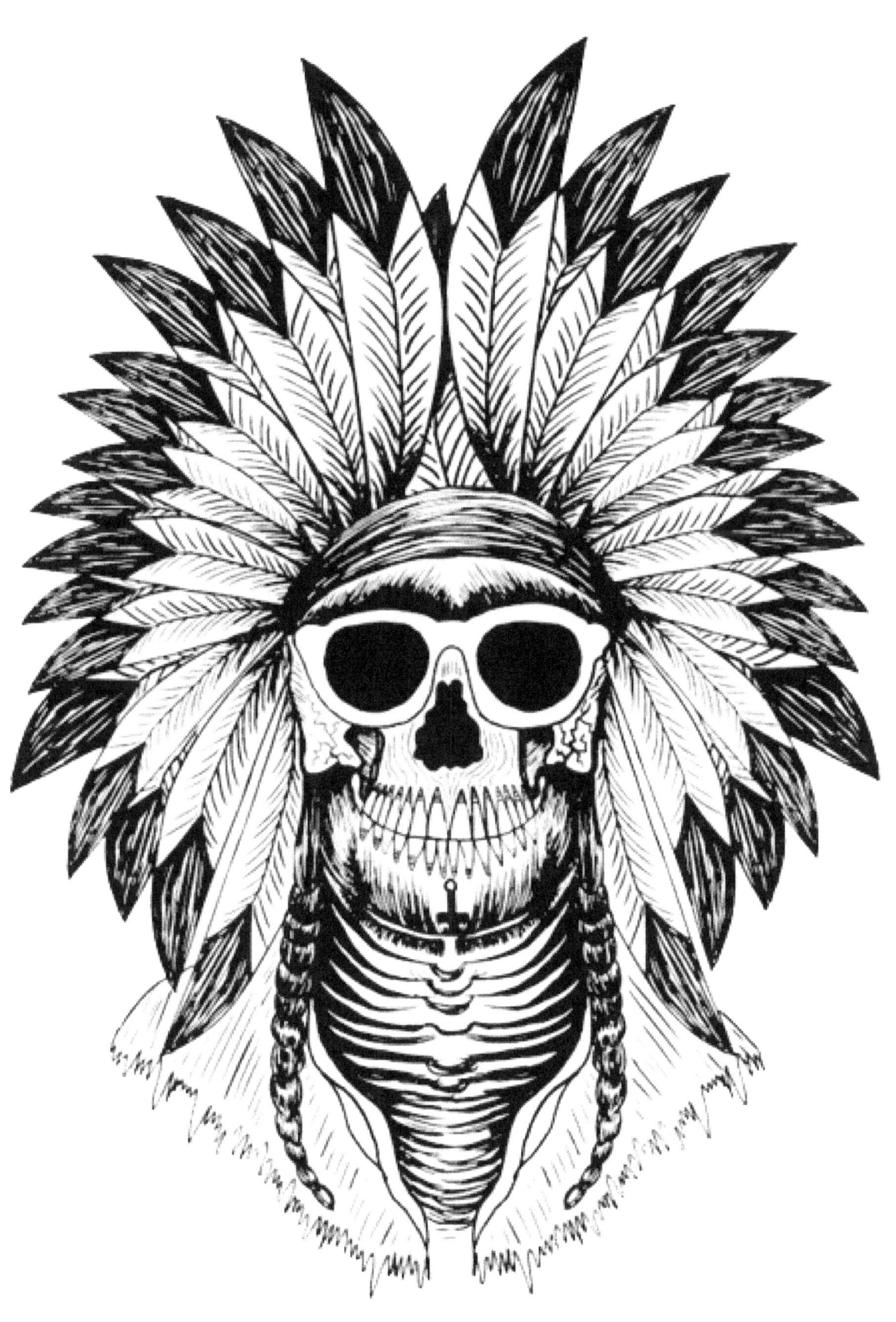

Coloring Test Pages

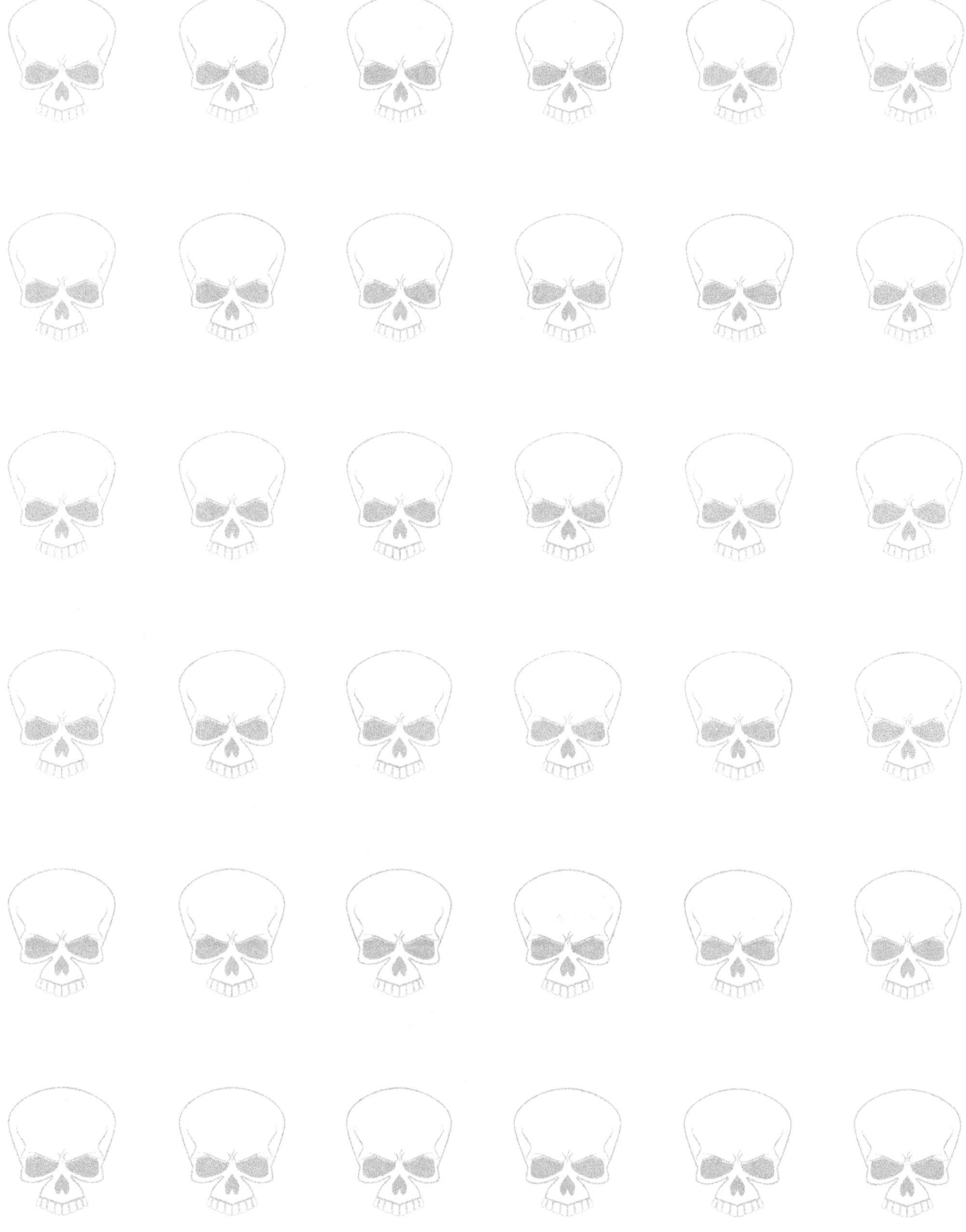

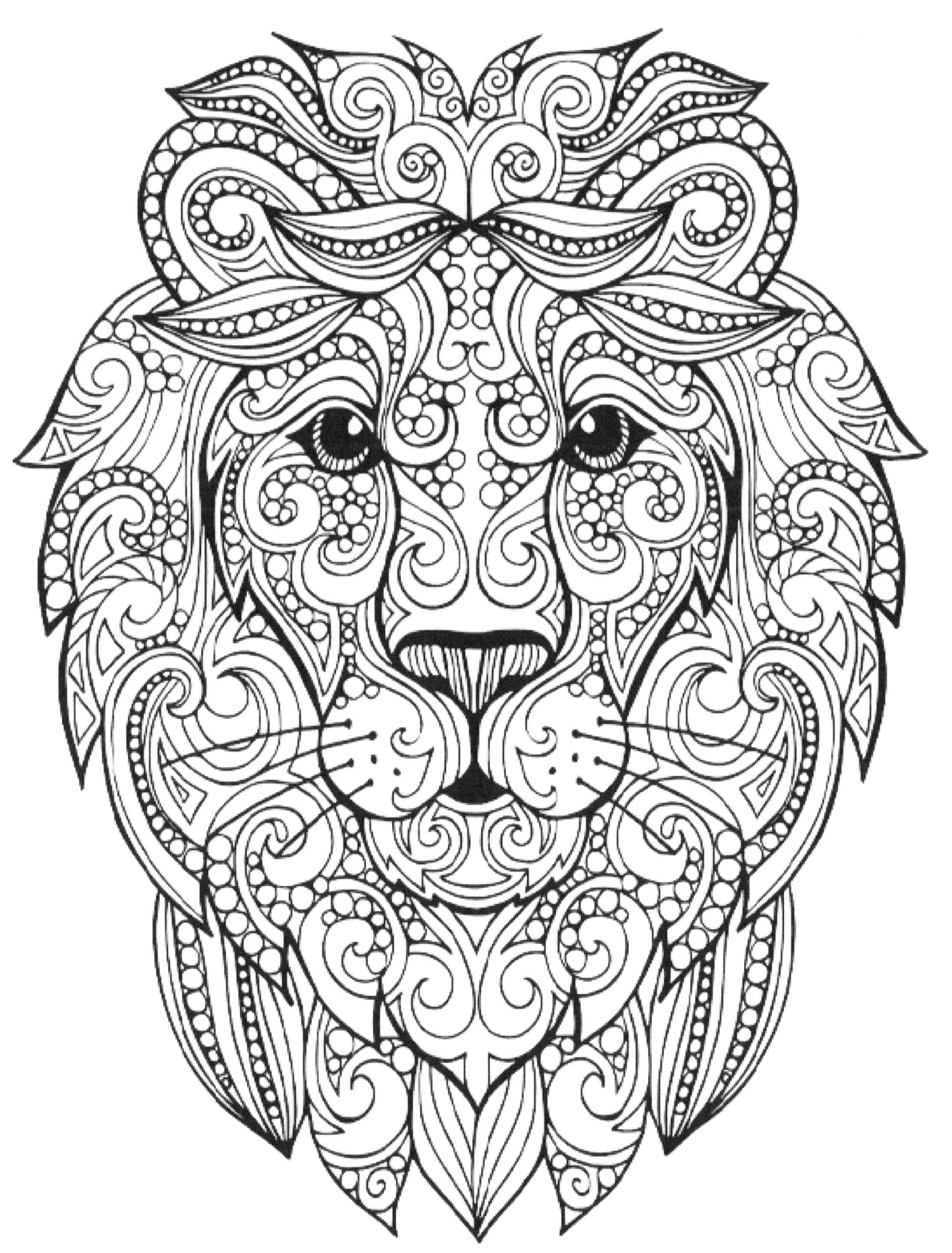

Coloring Test Pages

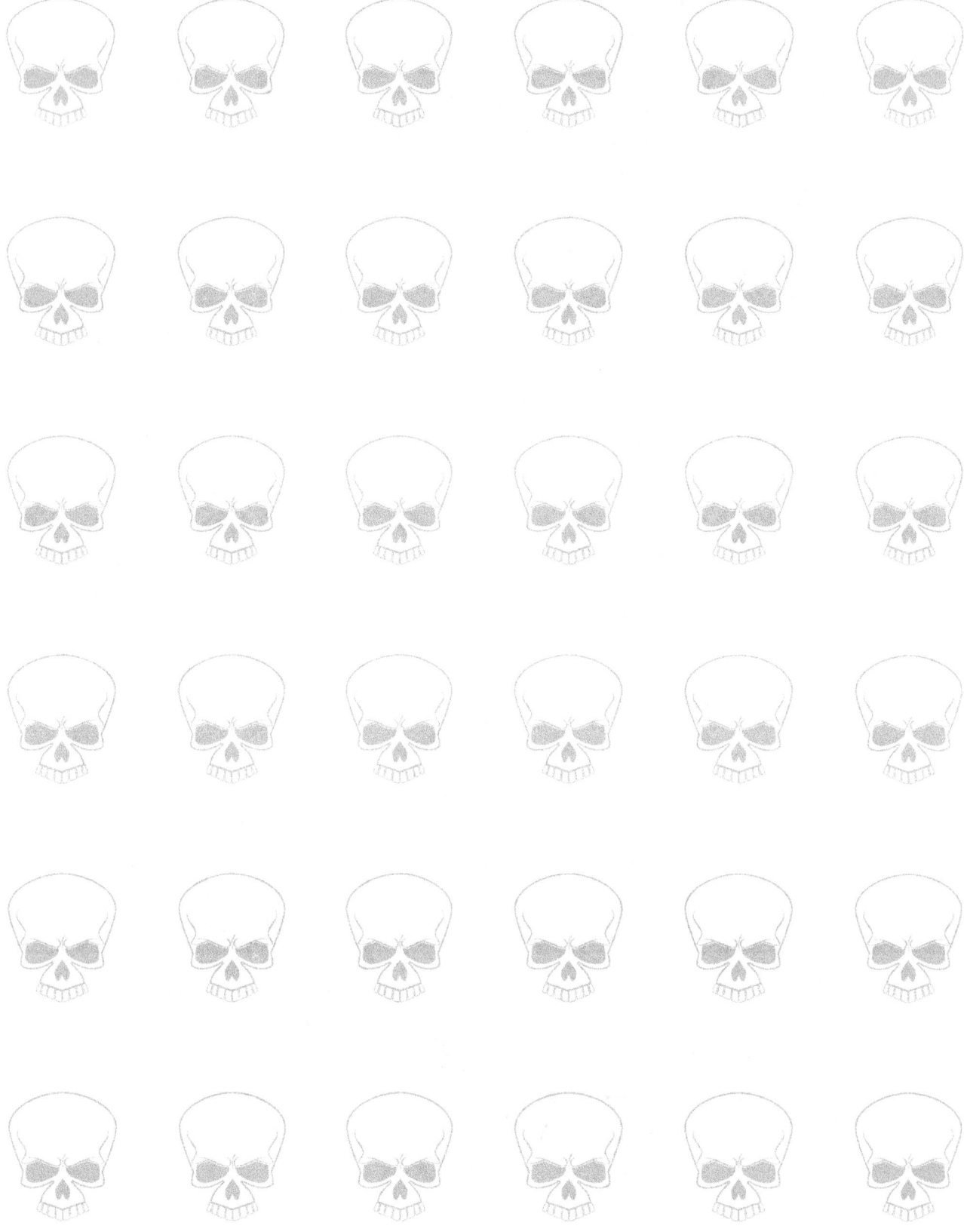

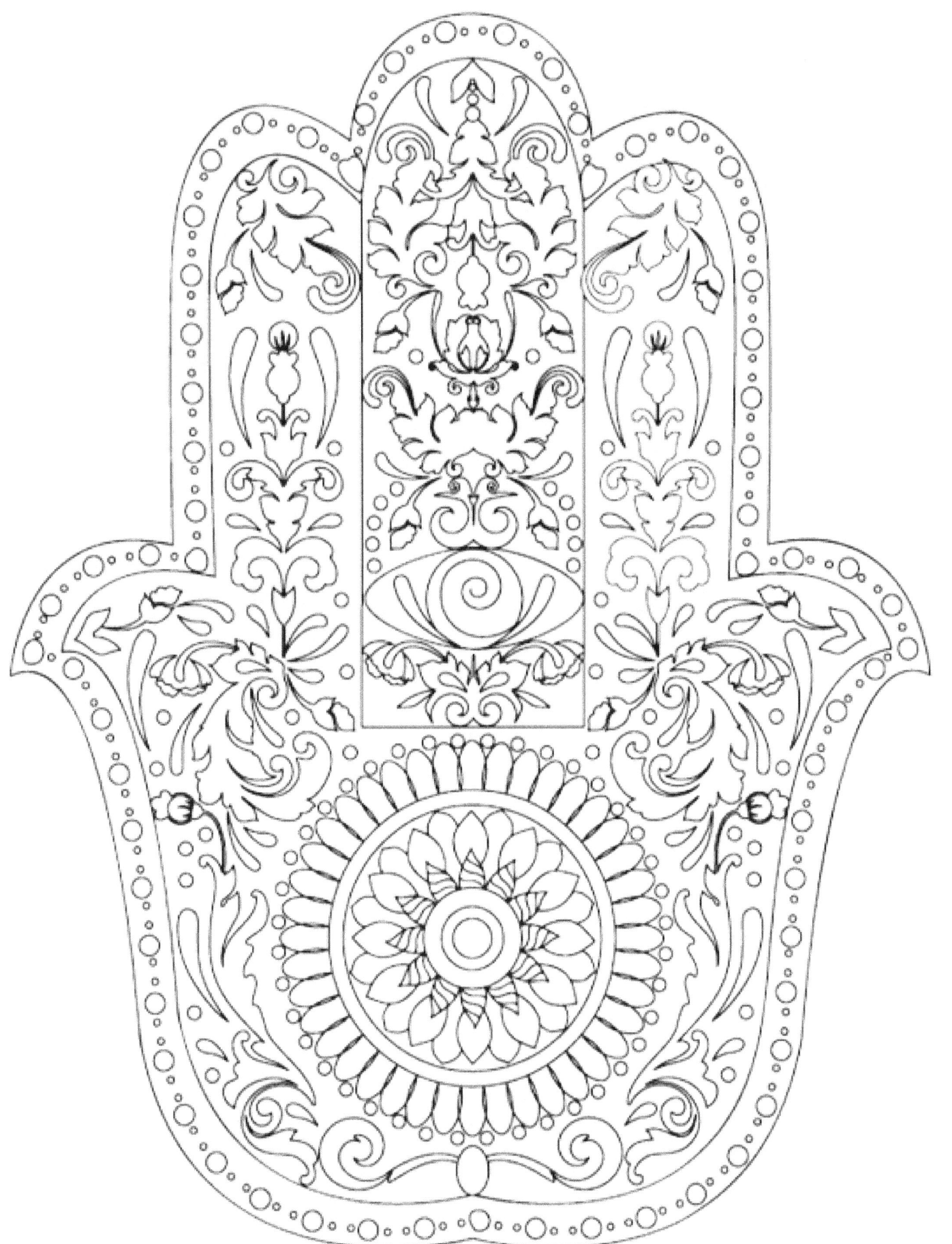

Coloring Test Pages

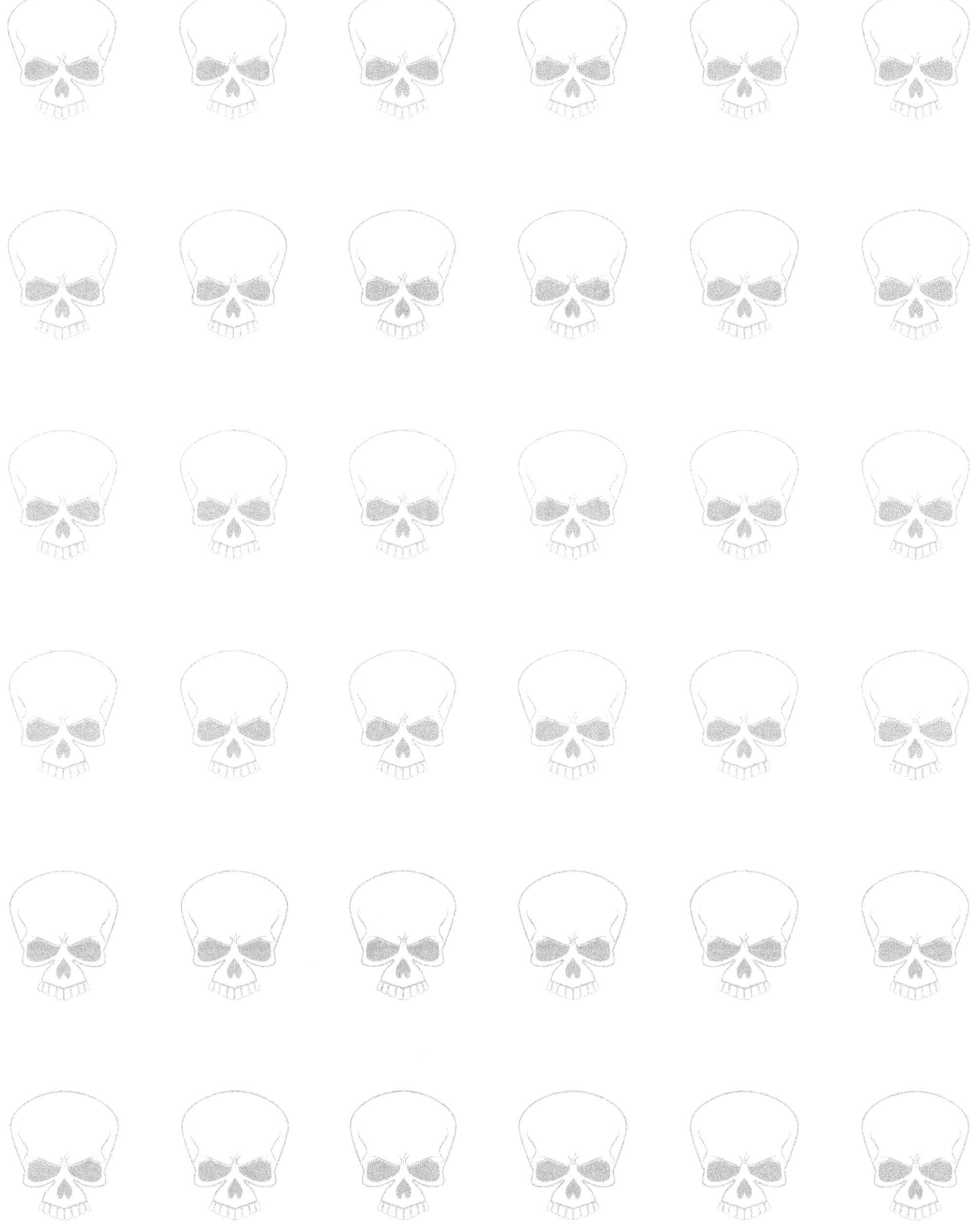

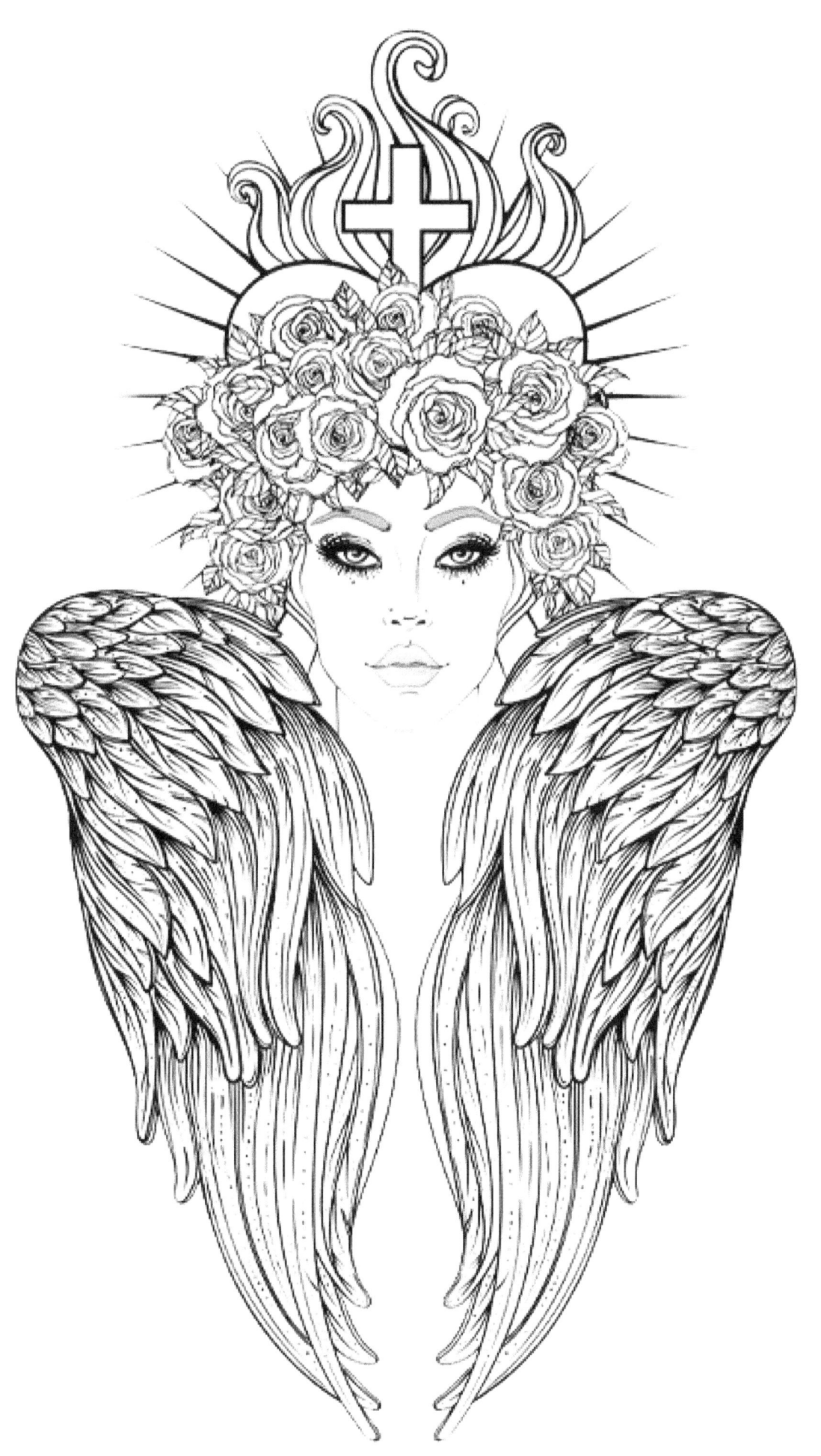

Coloring Test Pages

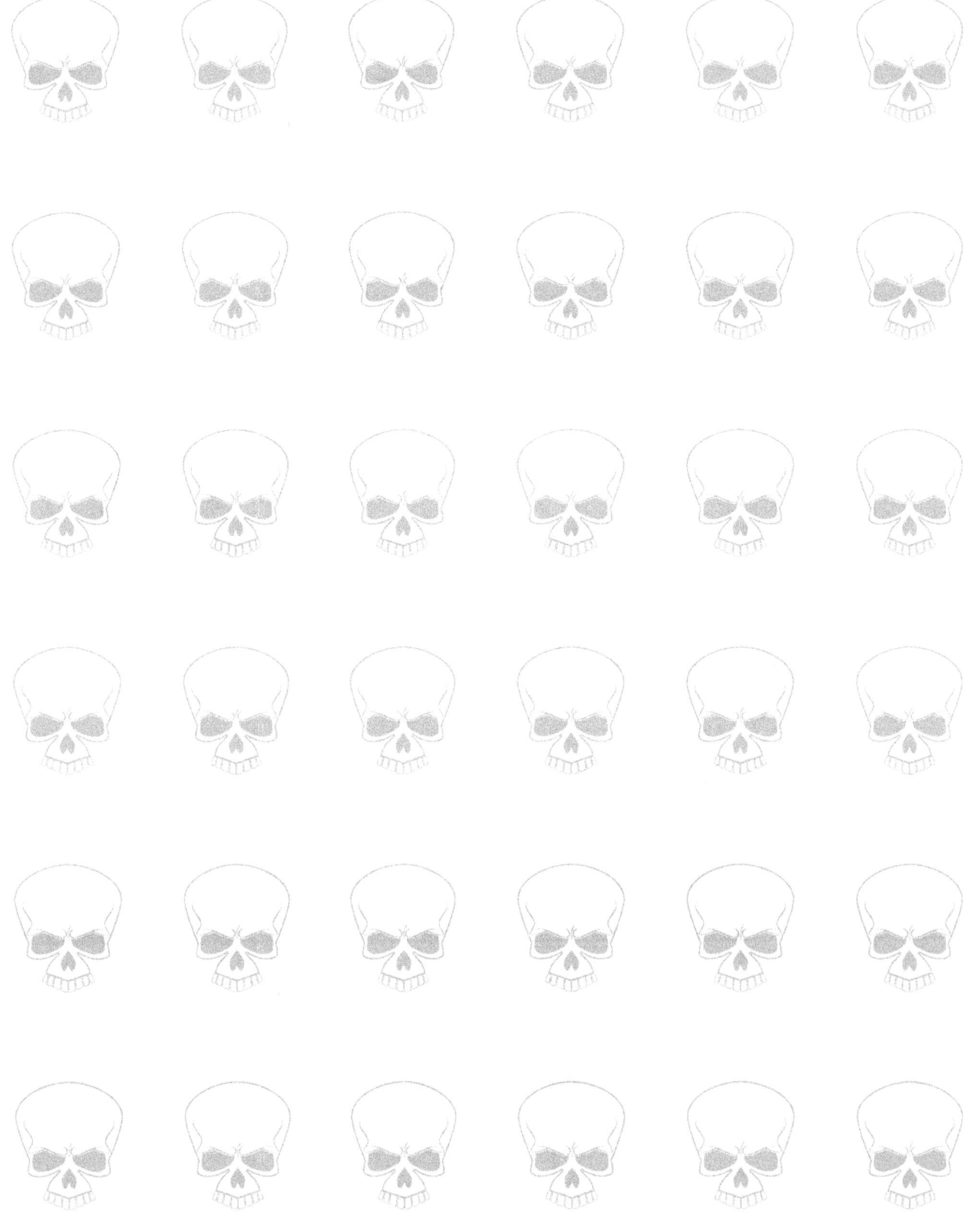

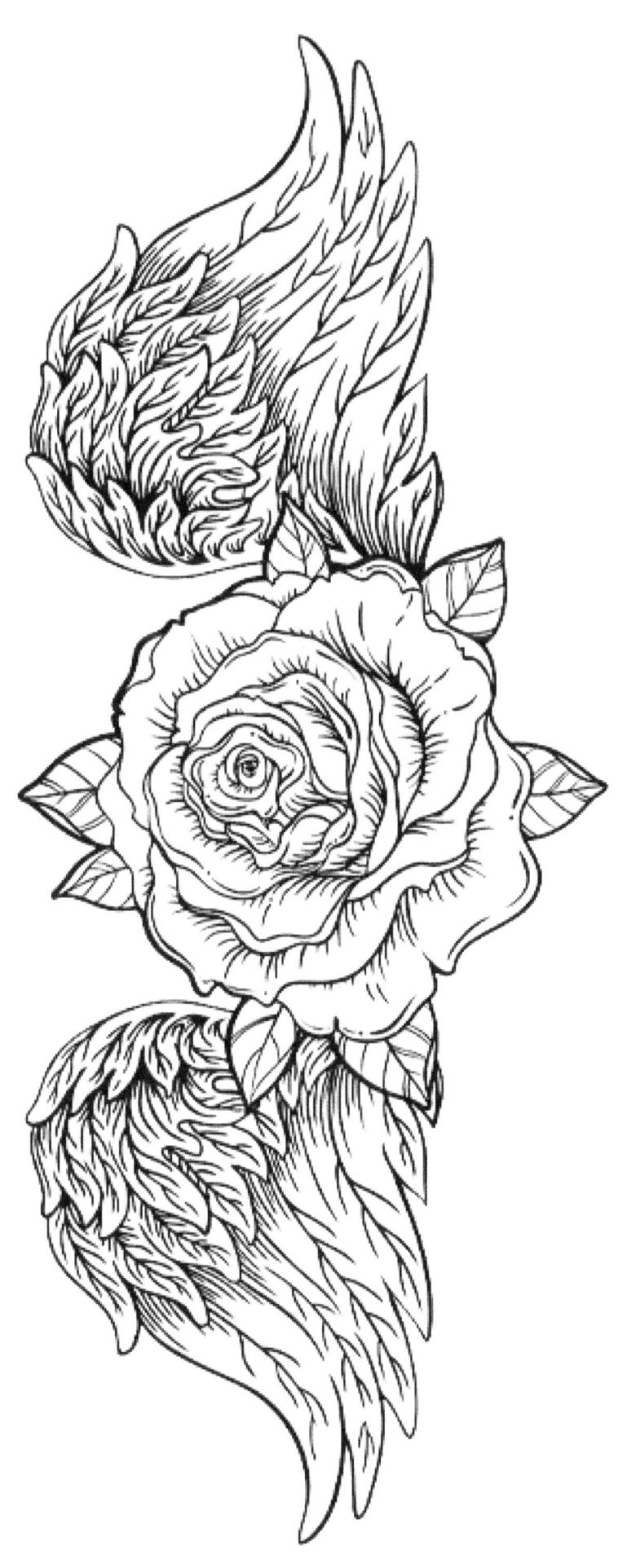

Coloring Test Pages

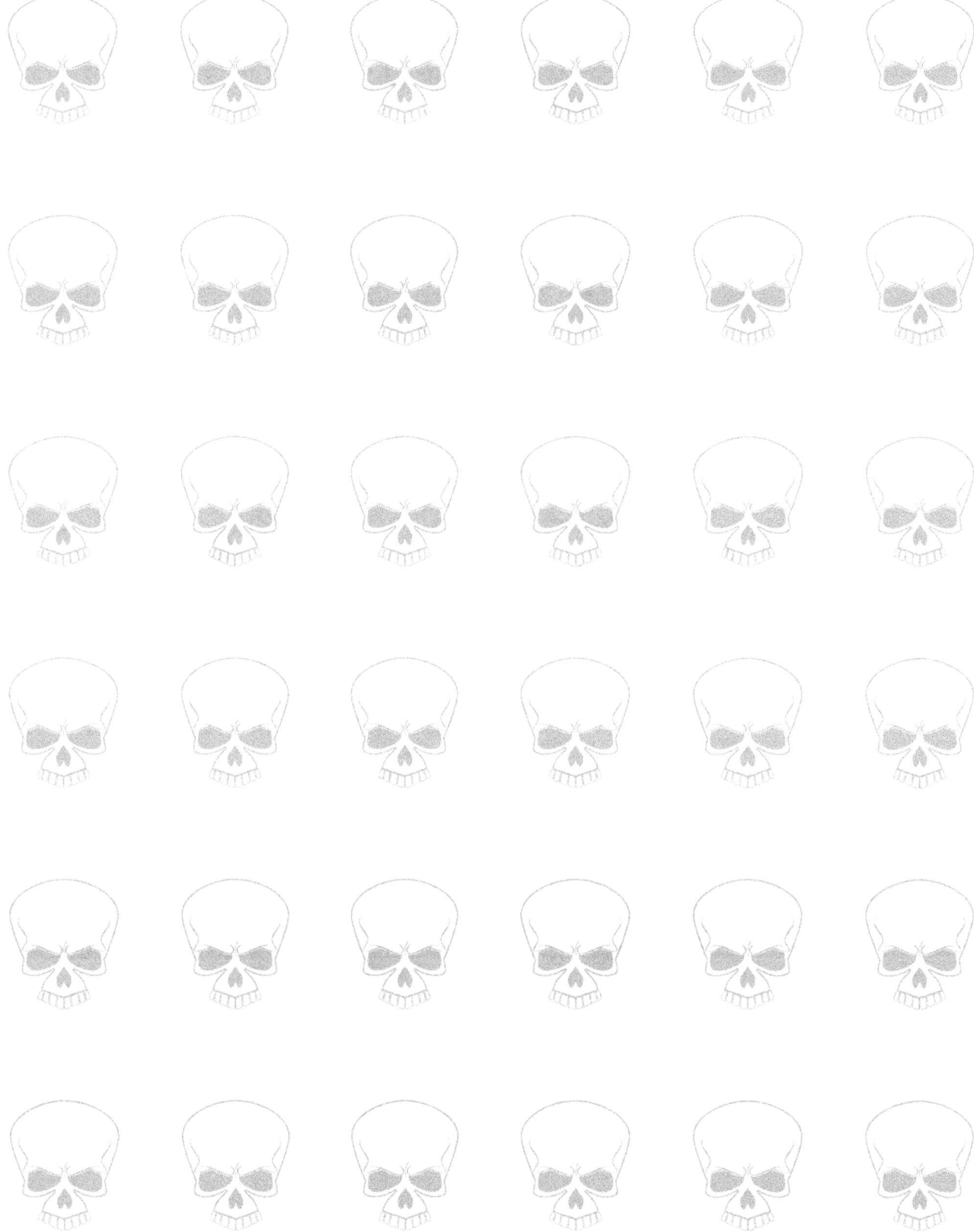

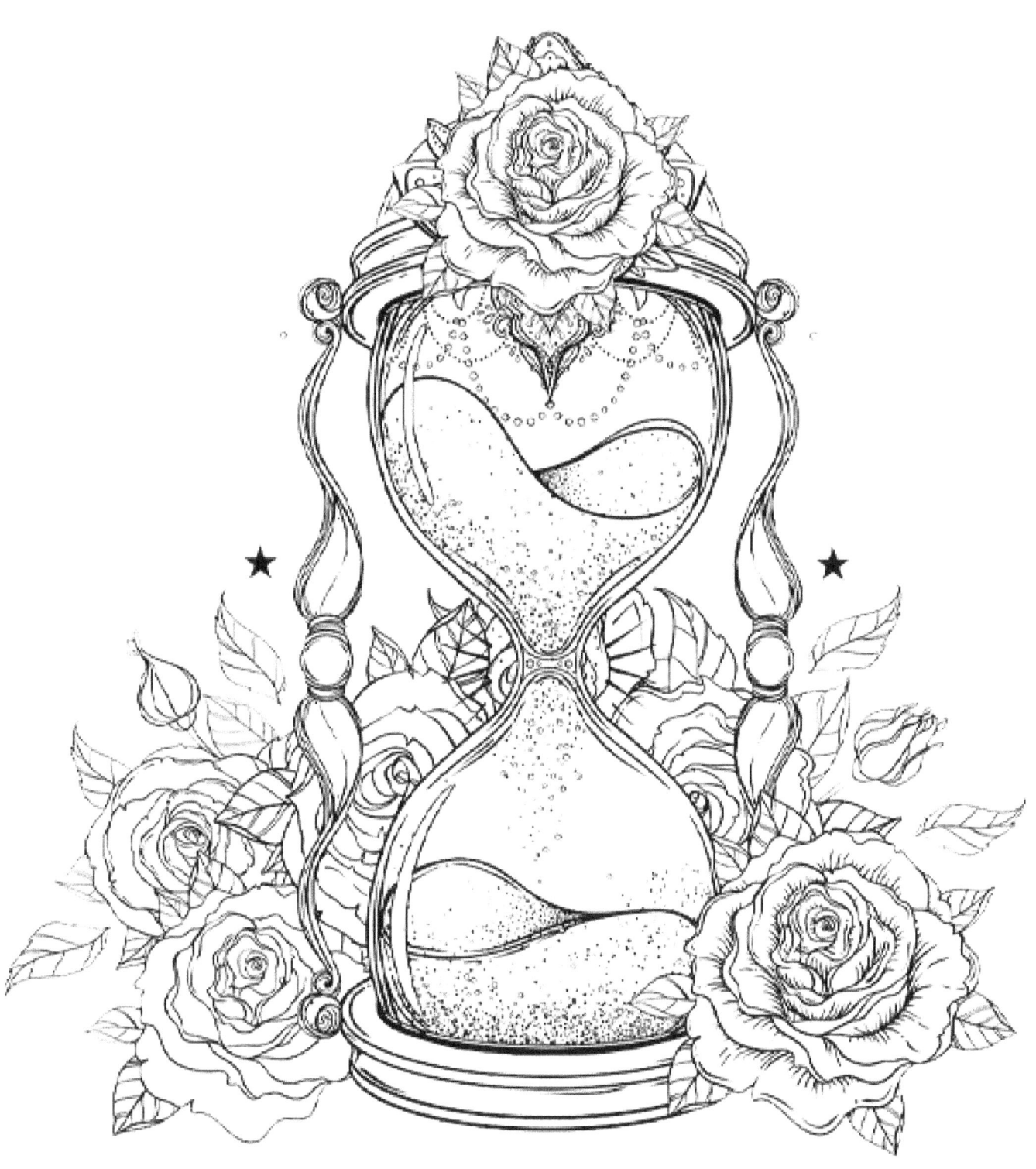

Coloring Test Pages

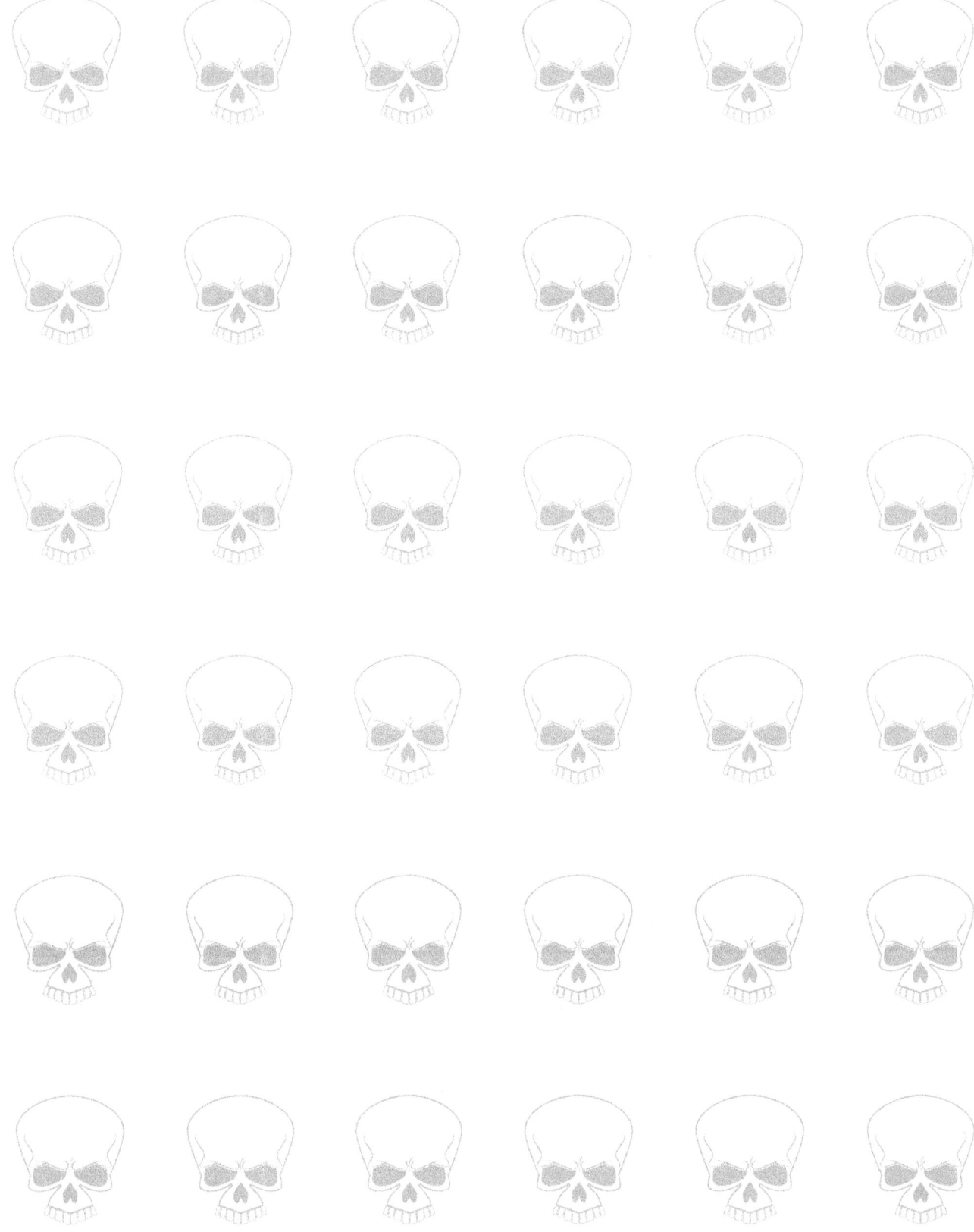

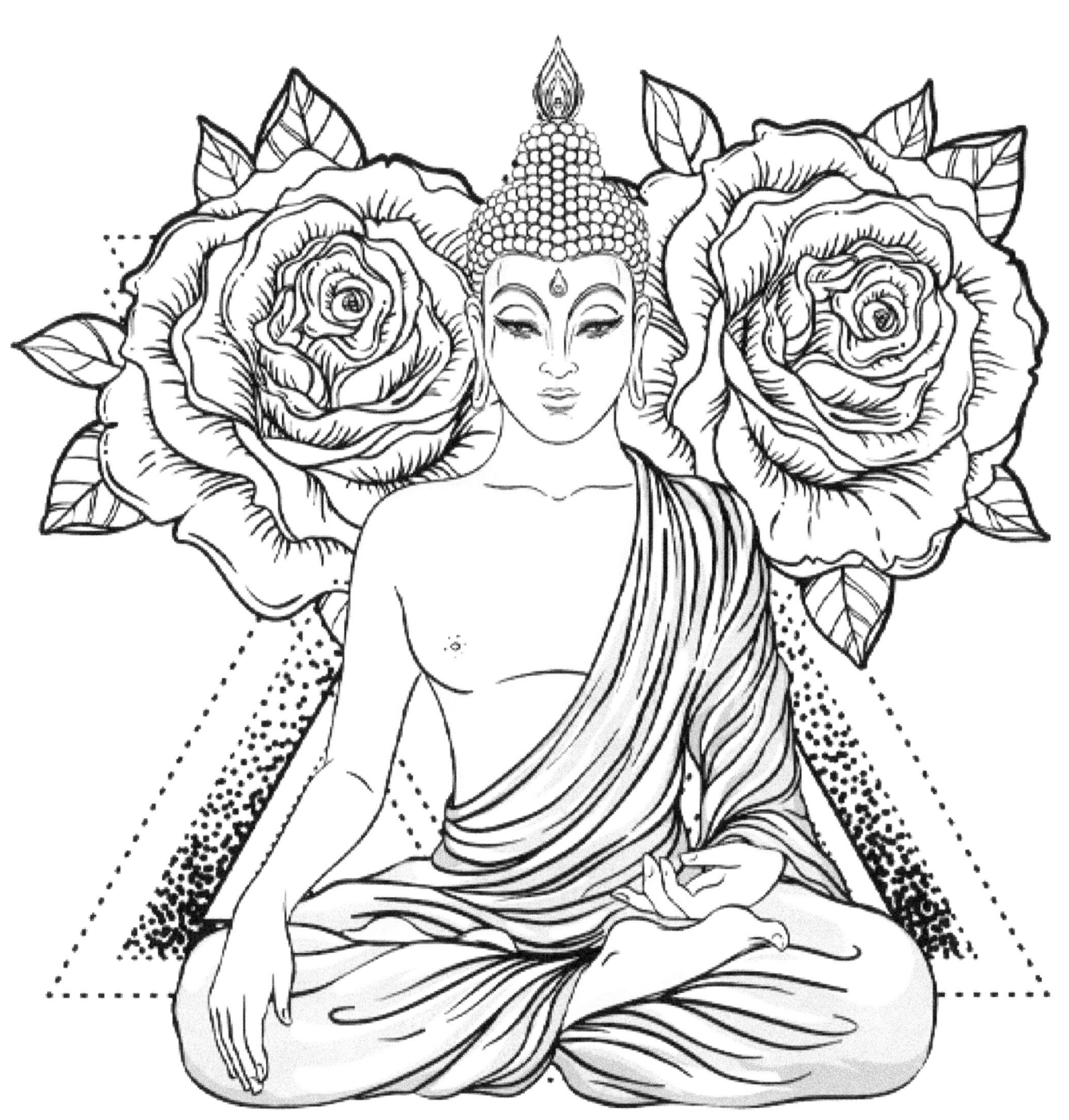

Coloring Test Pages

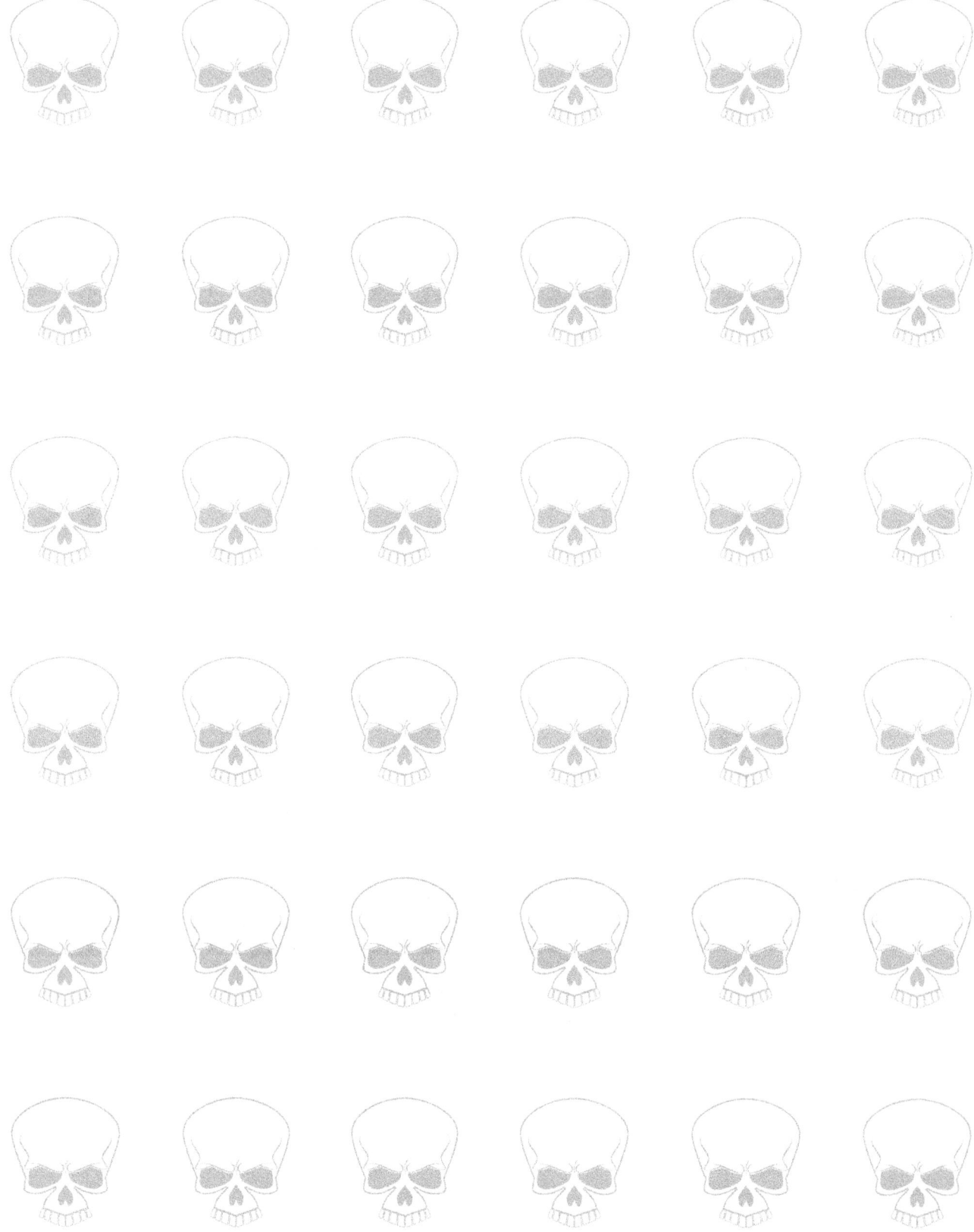

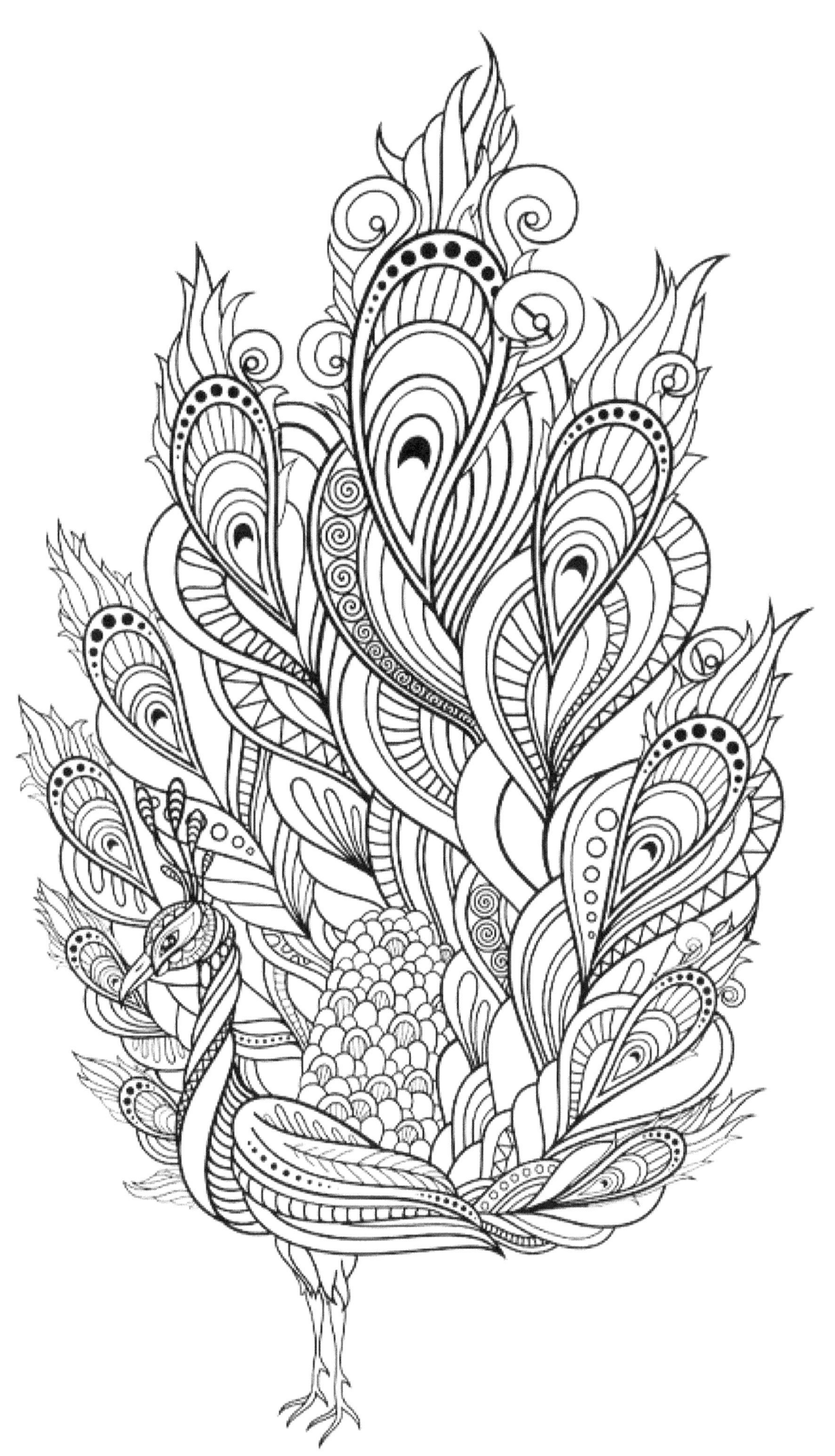

Coloring Test Pages

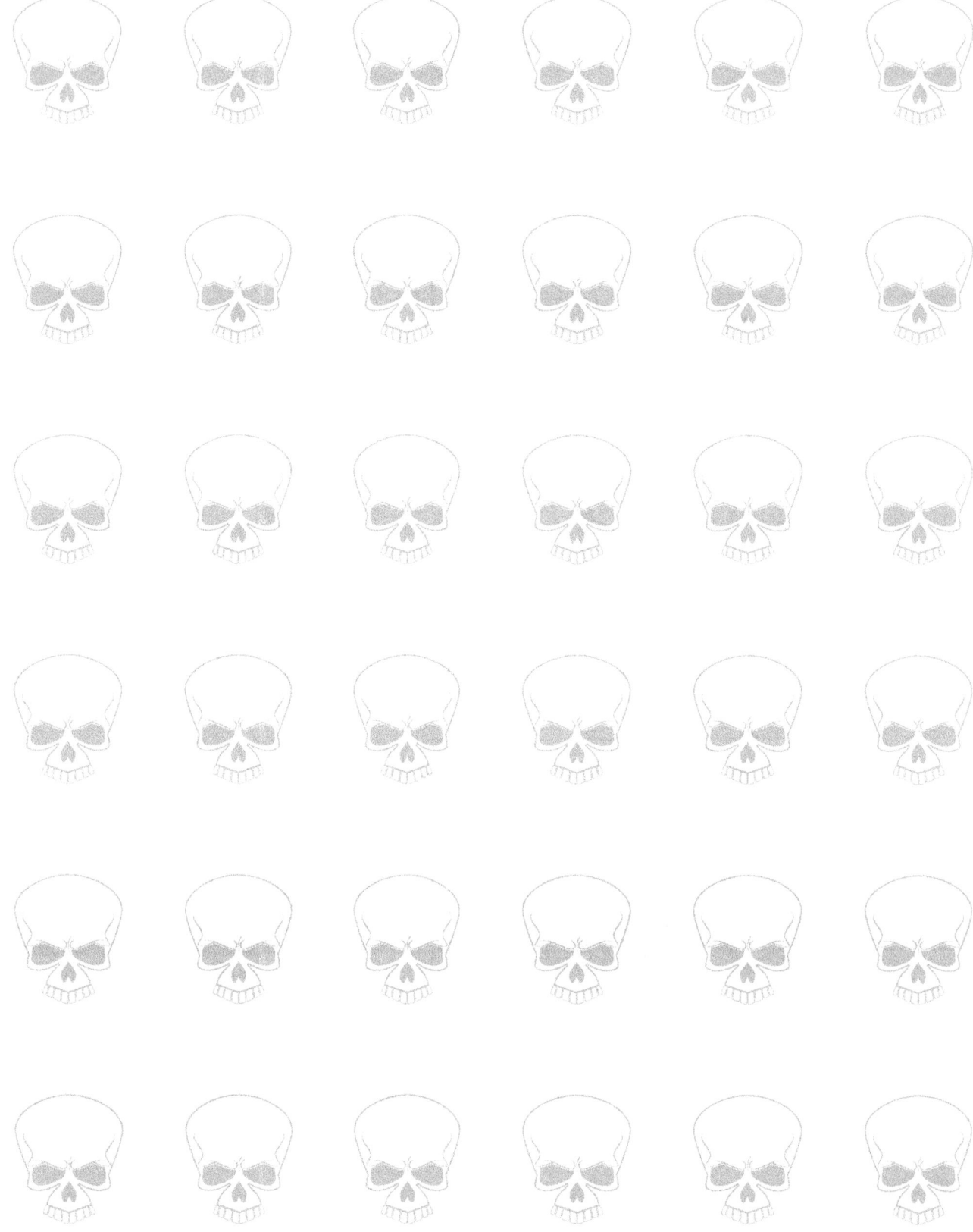

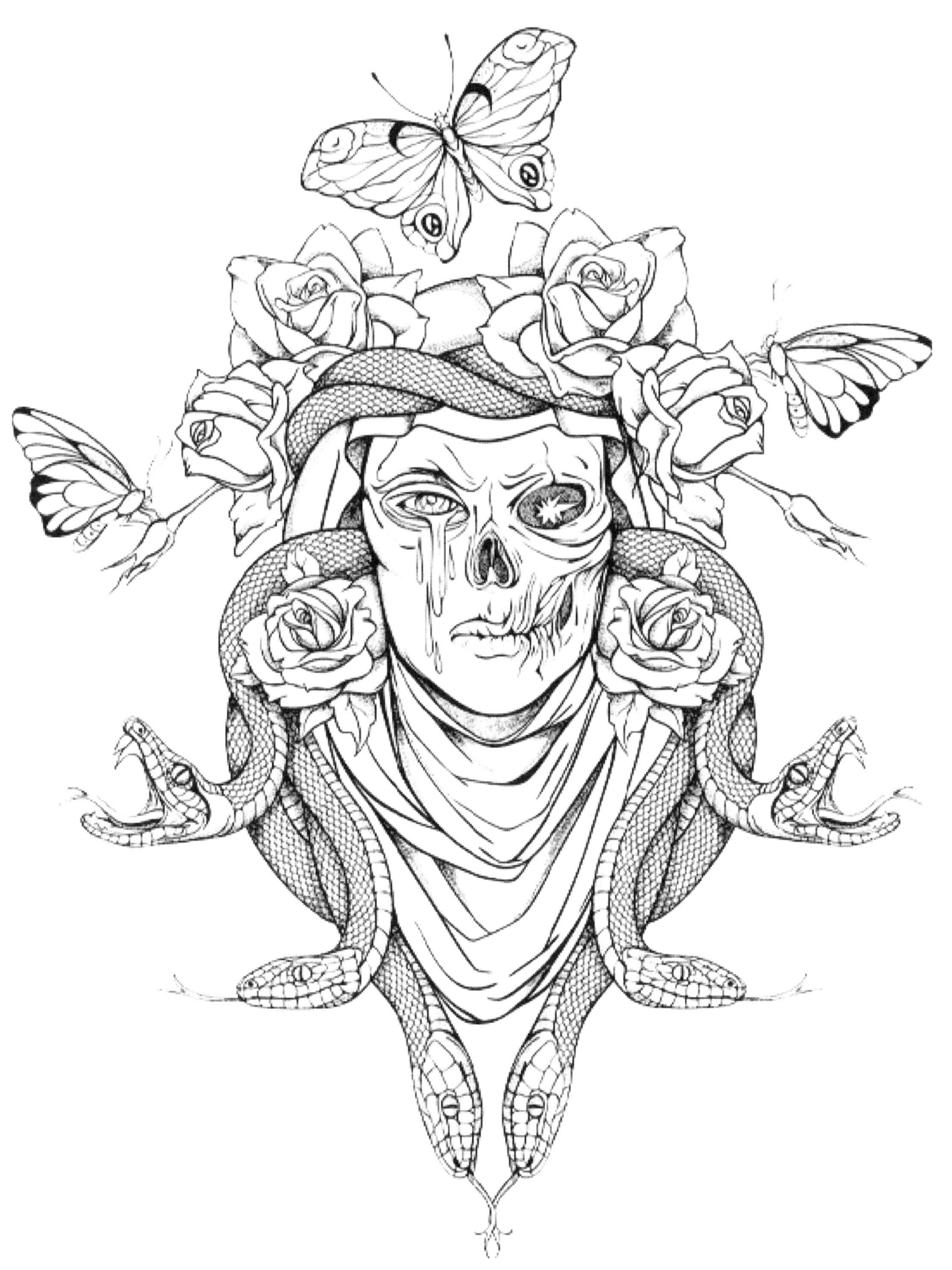

Coloring Test Pages

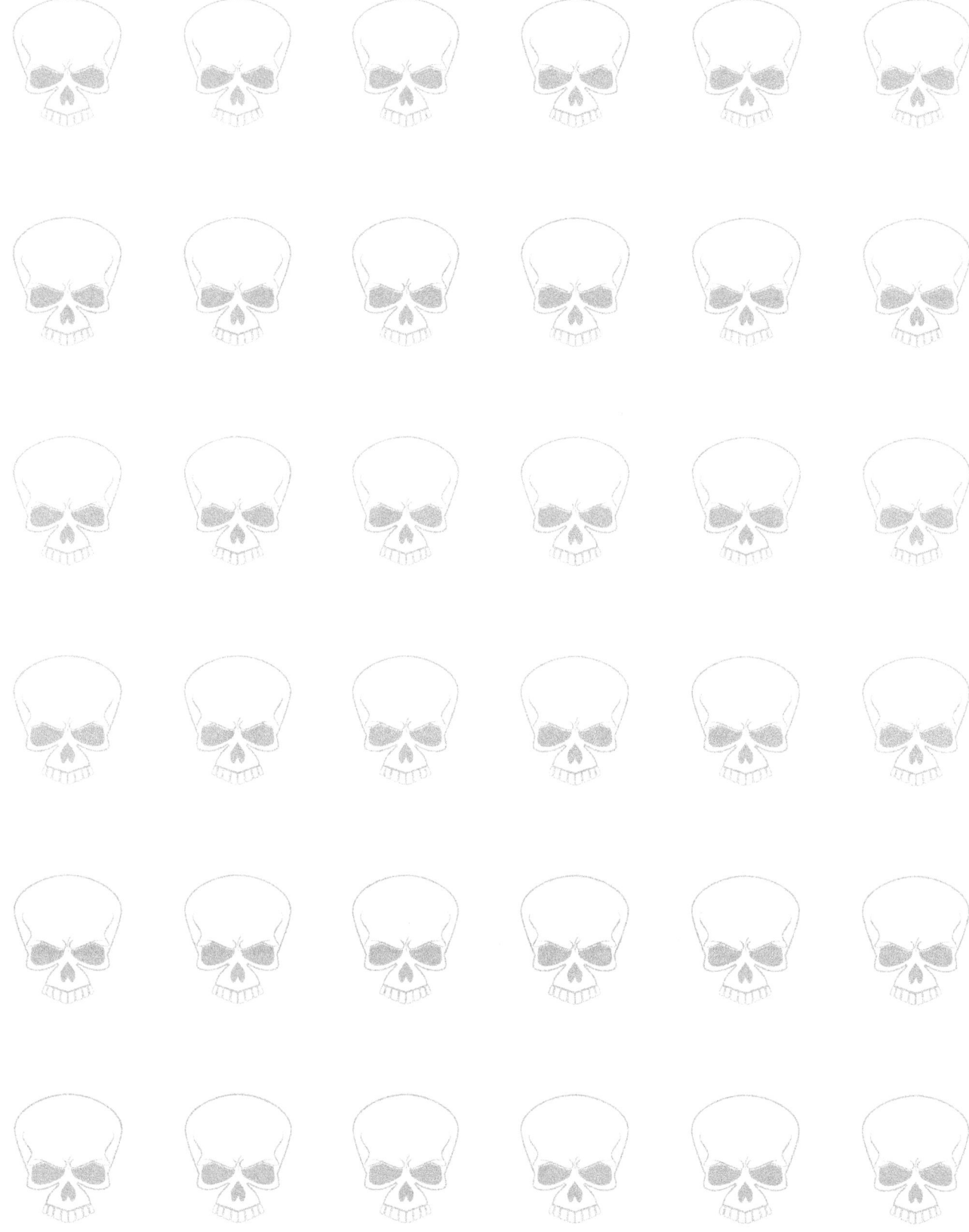

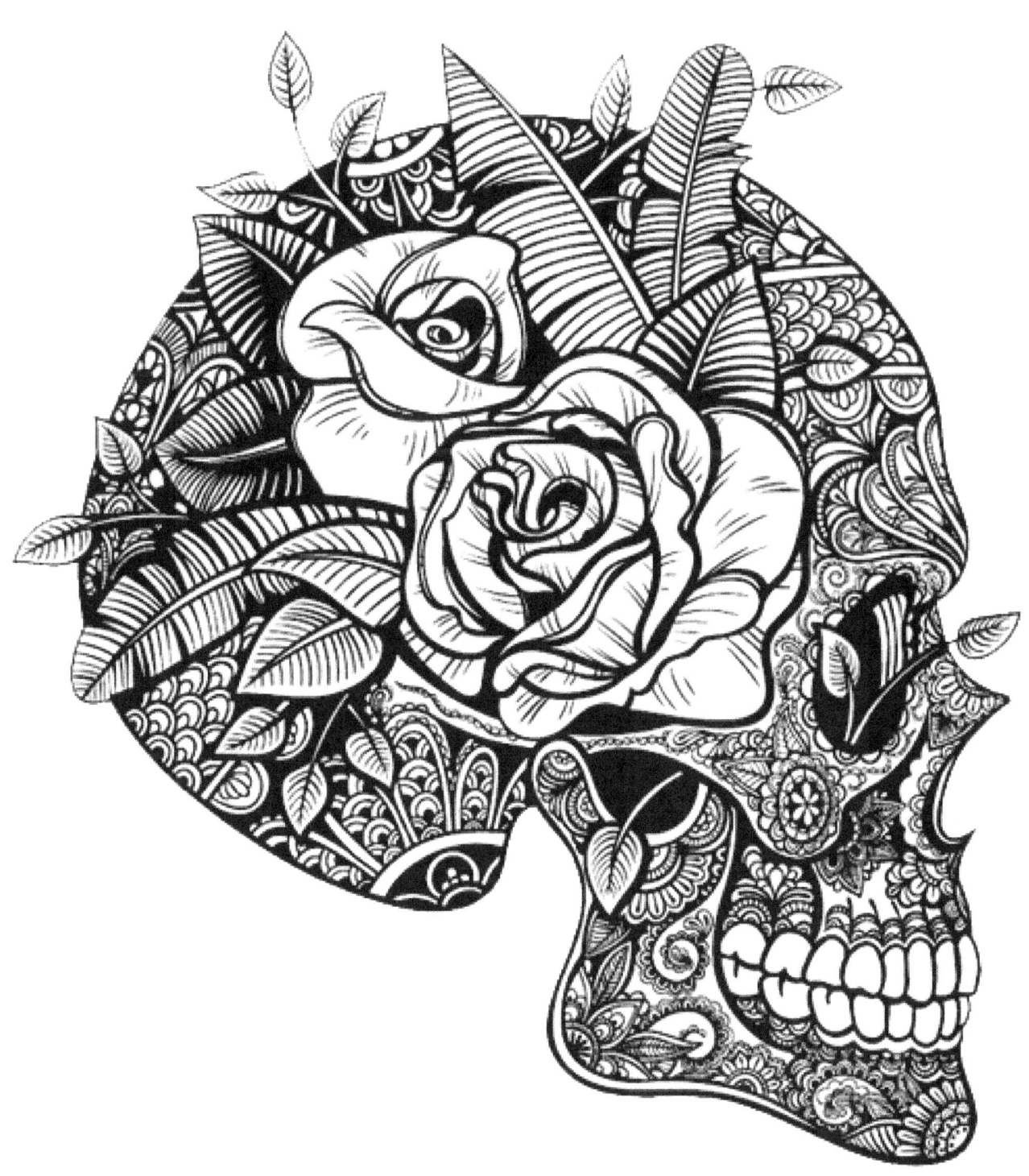

Coloring Test Pages

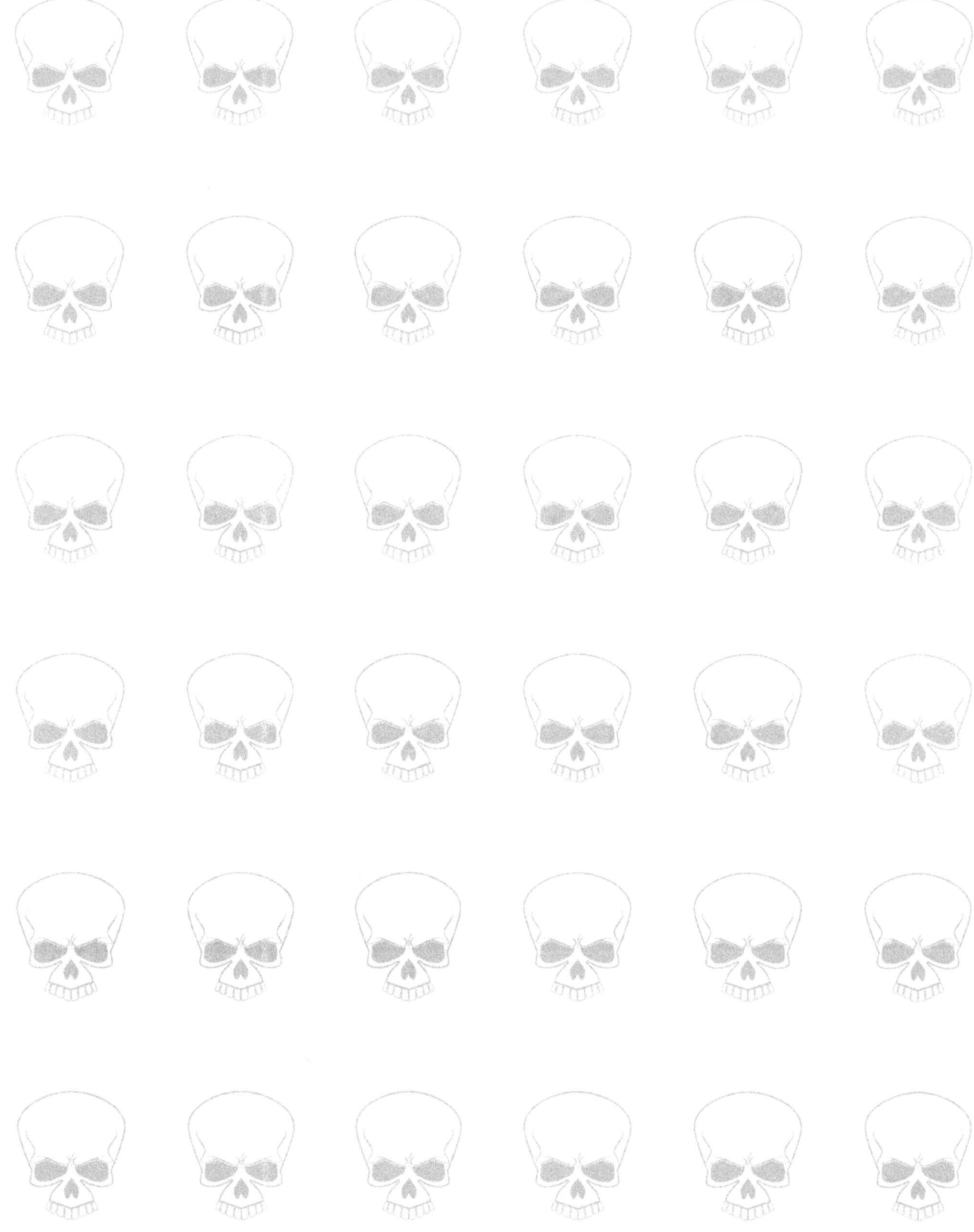

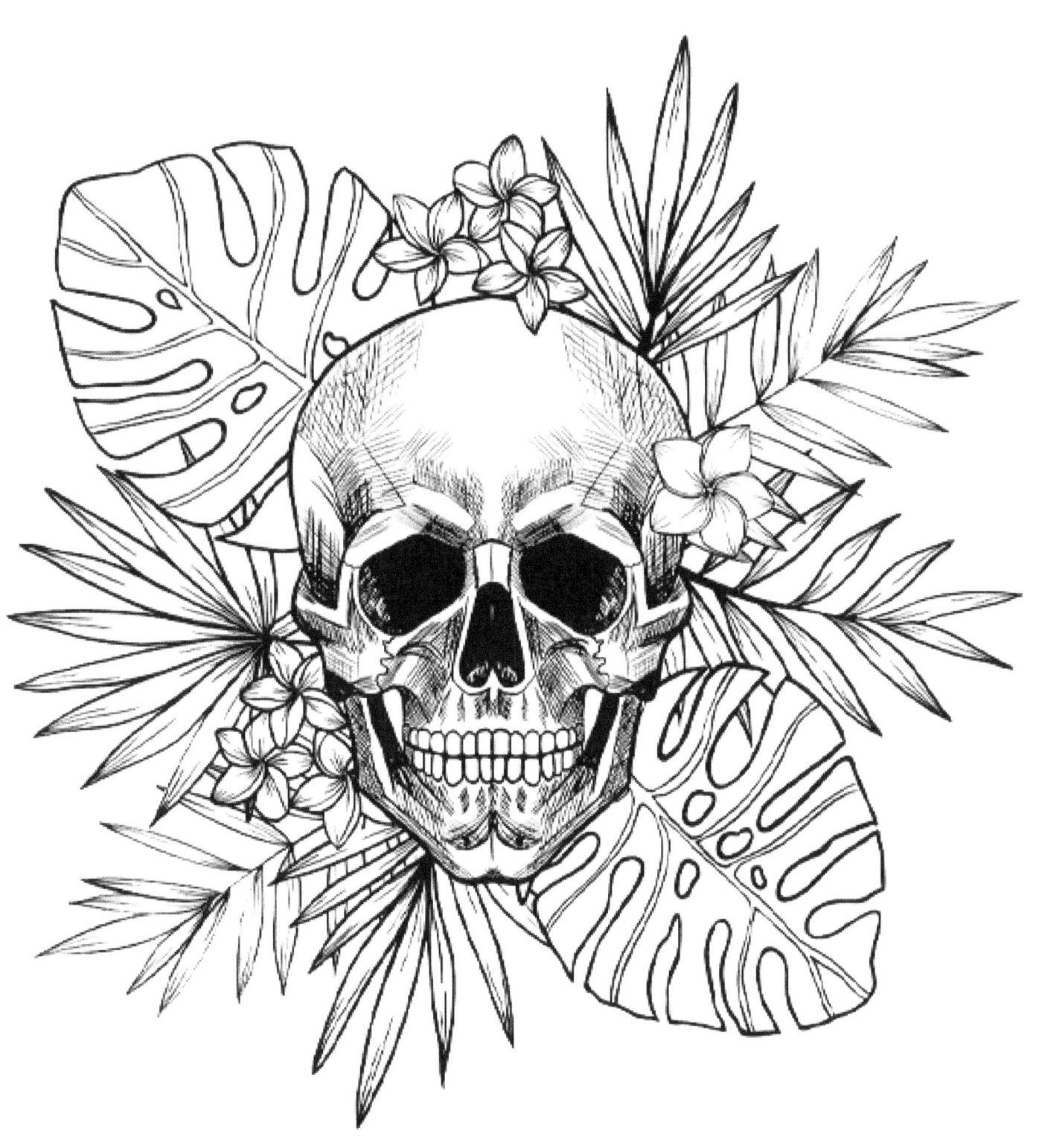

Coloring Test Pages

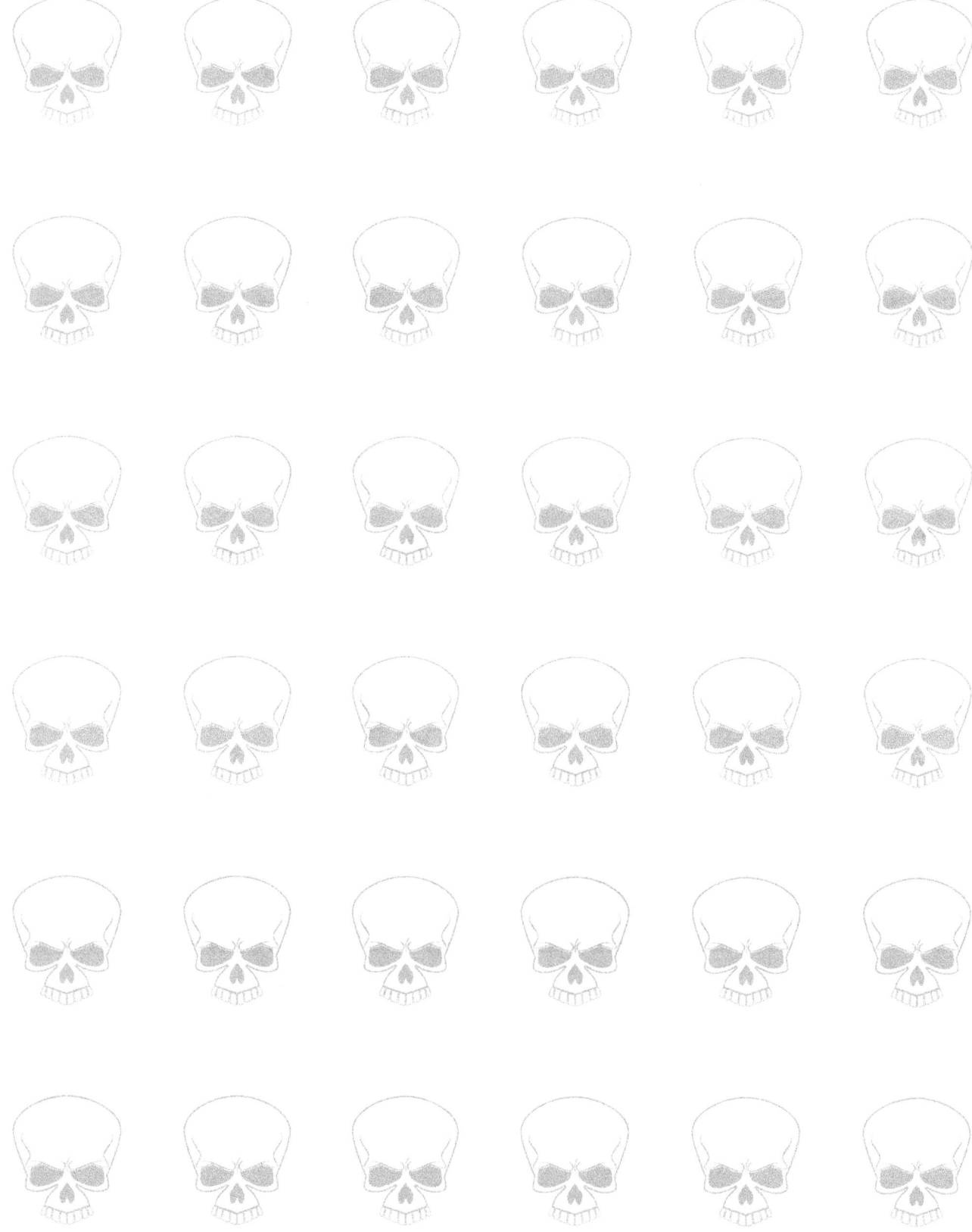

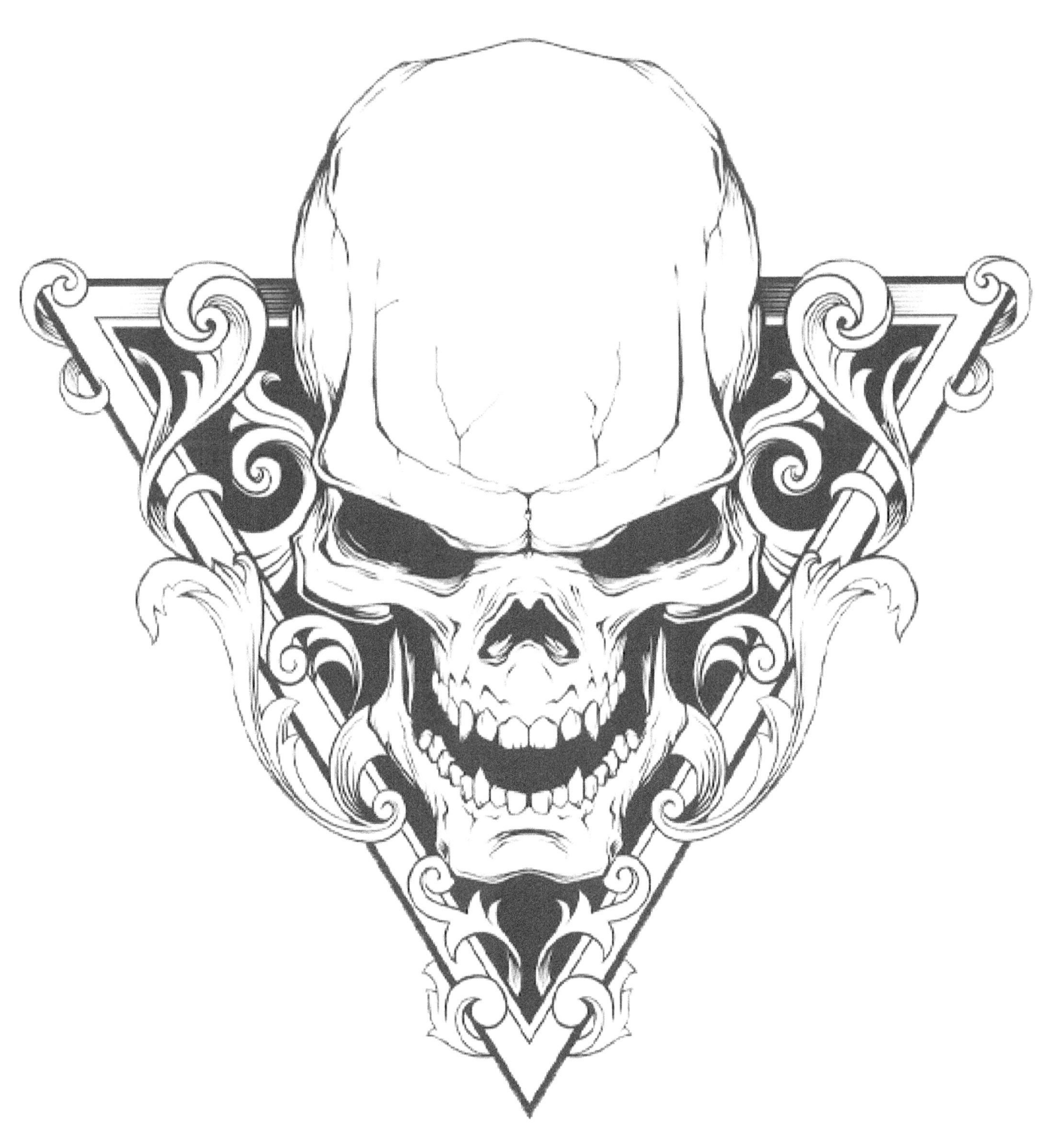

Coloring Test Pages

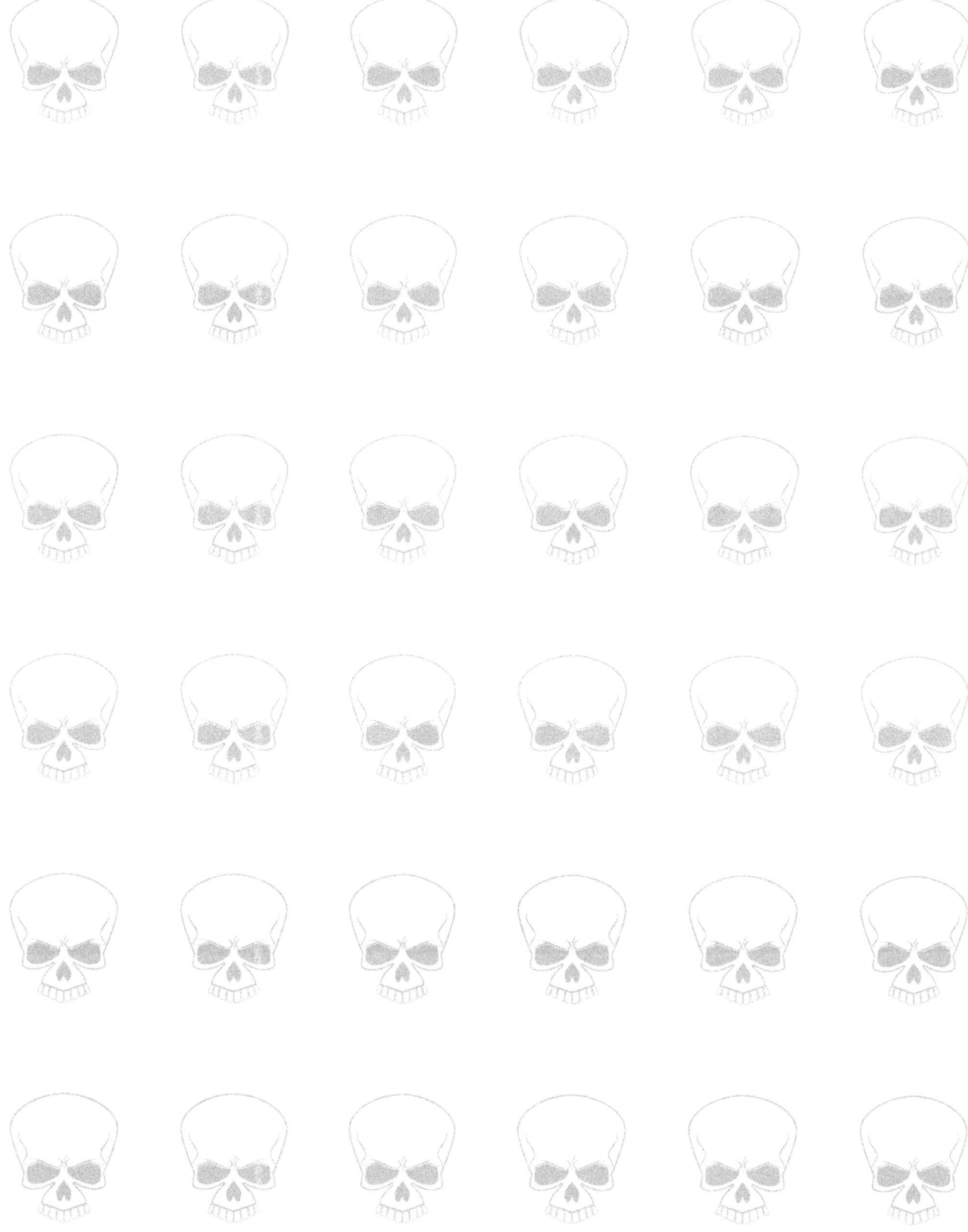

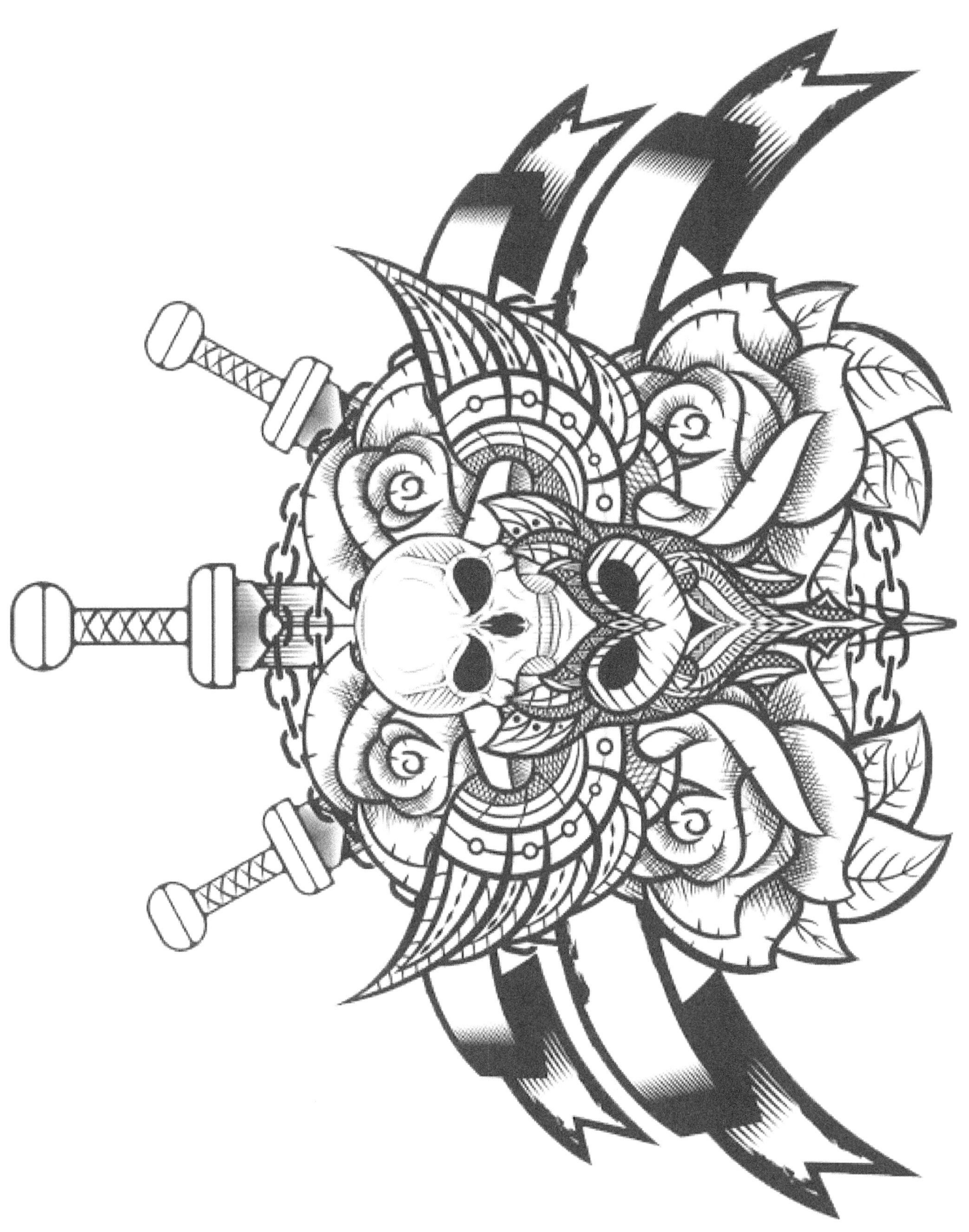

Coloring Test Pages

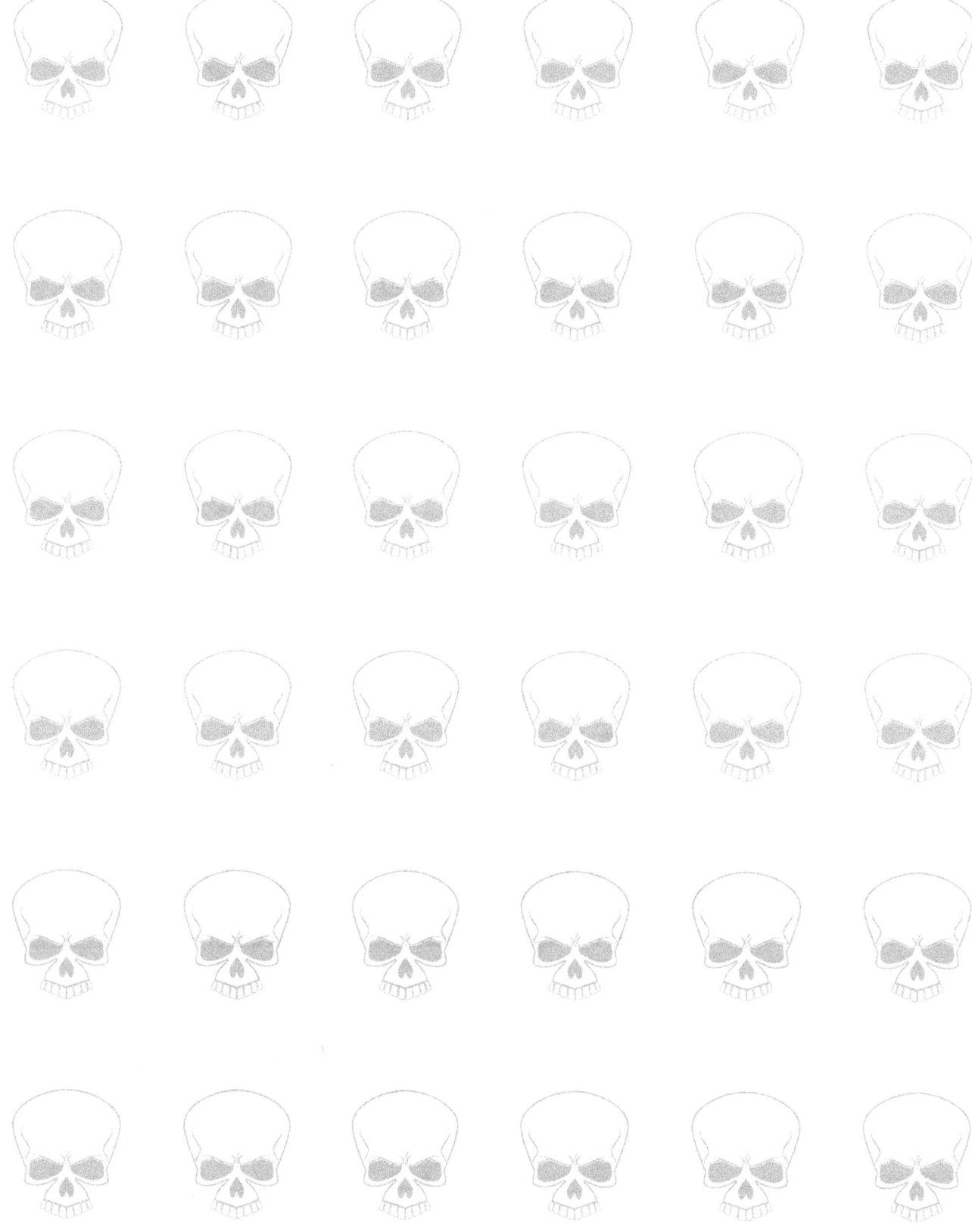

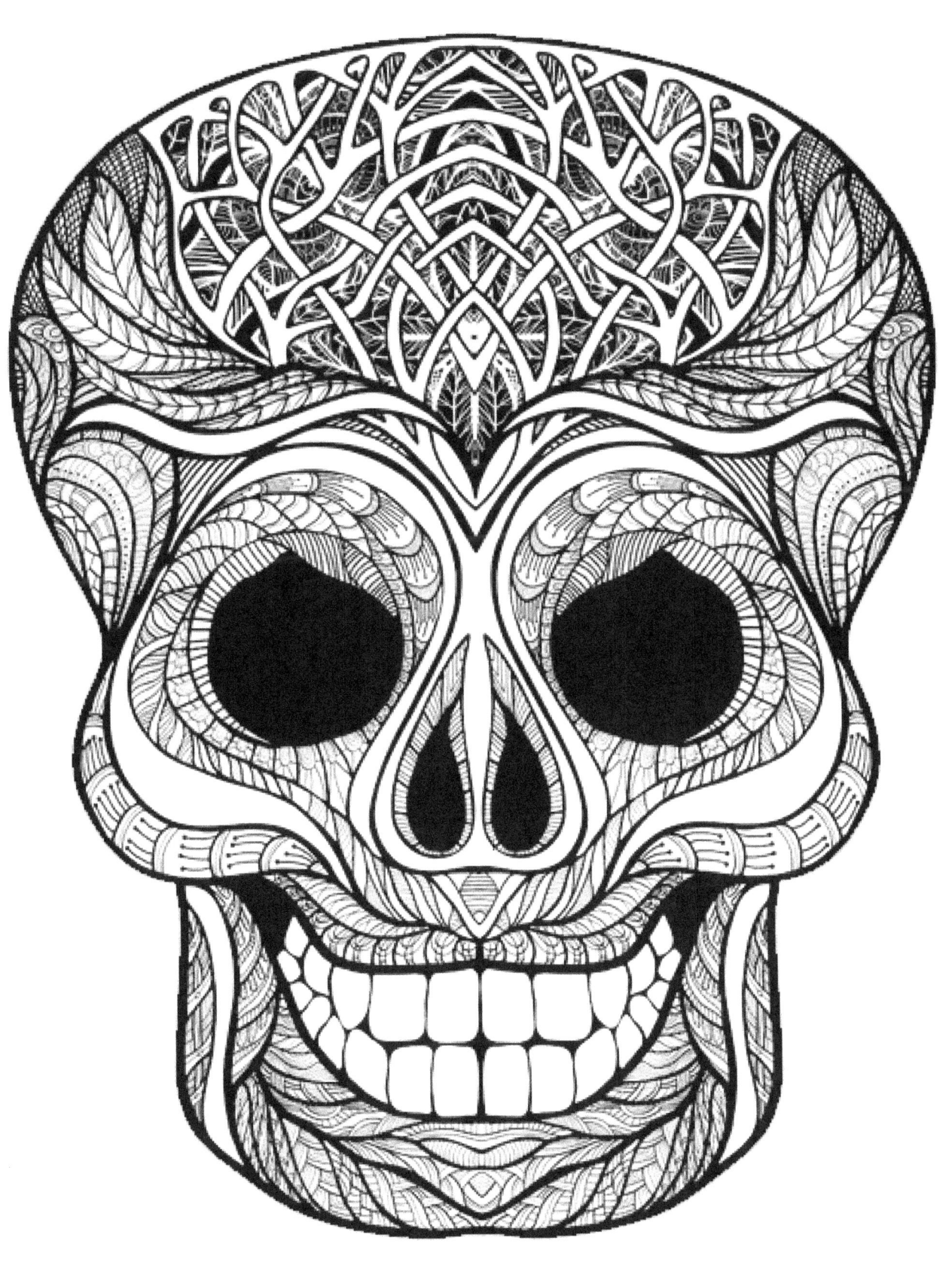

Coloring Test Pages

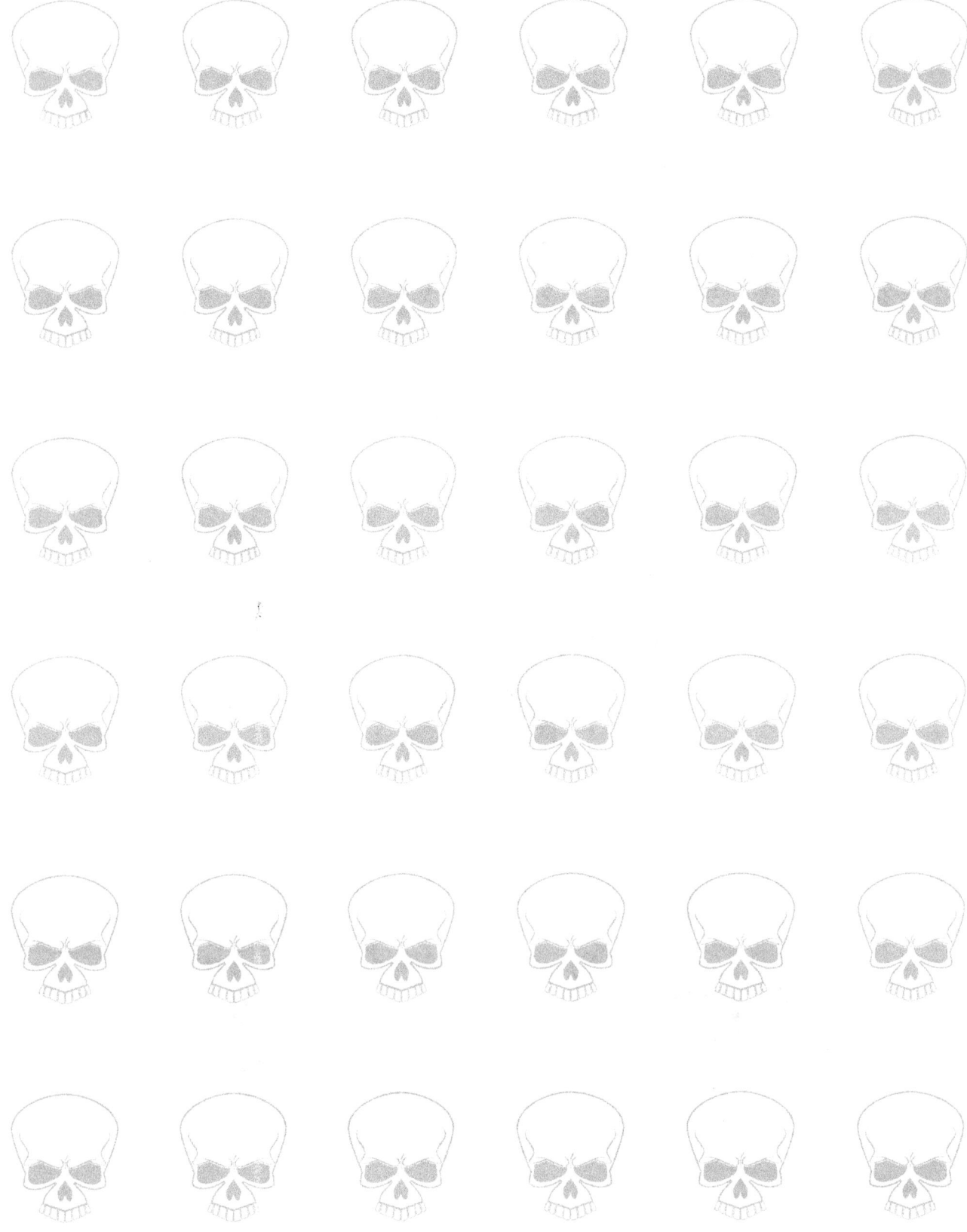

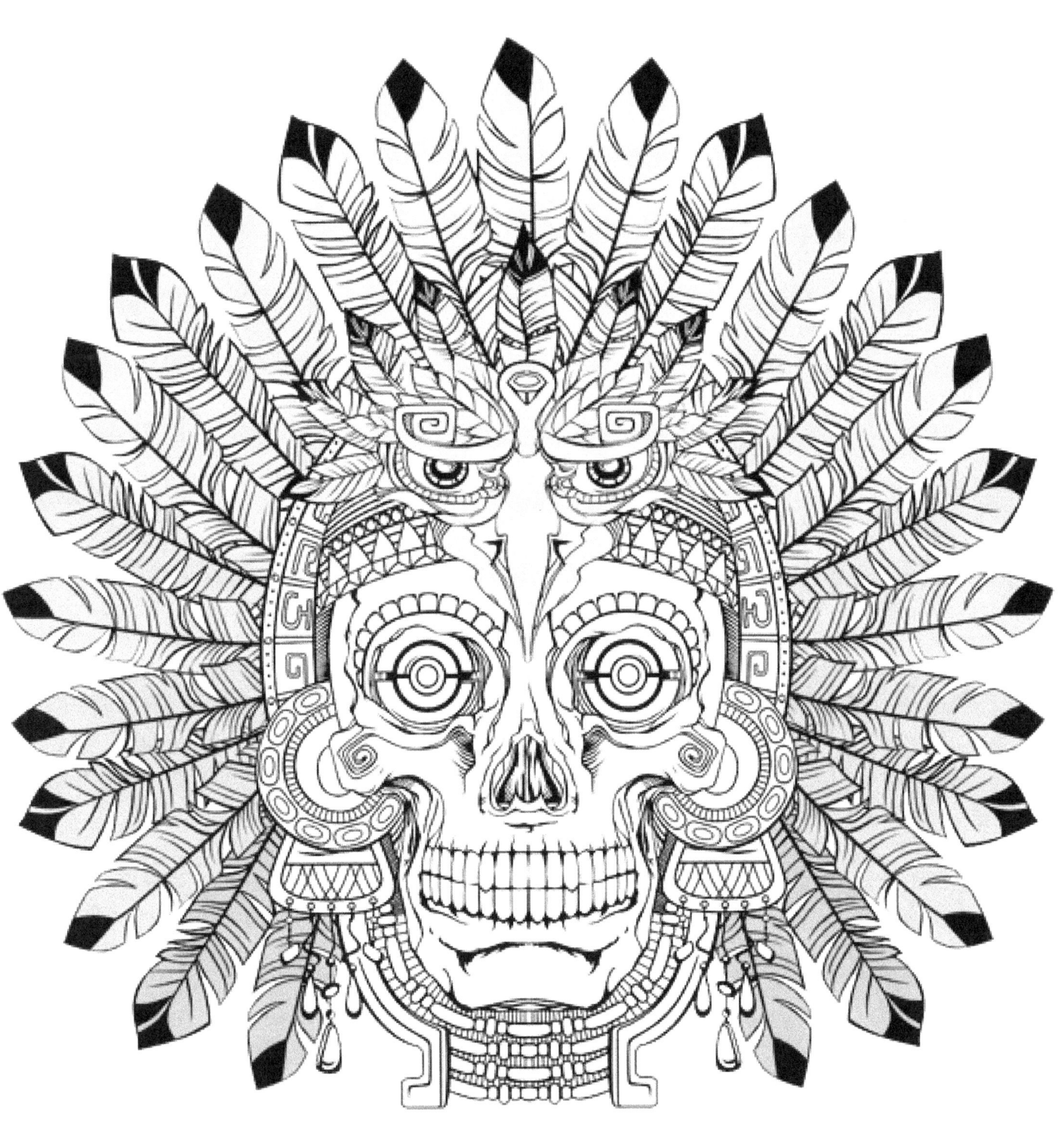

Coloring Test Pages

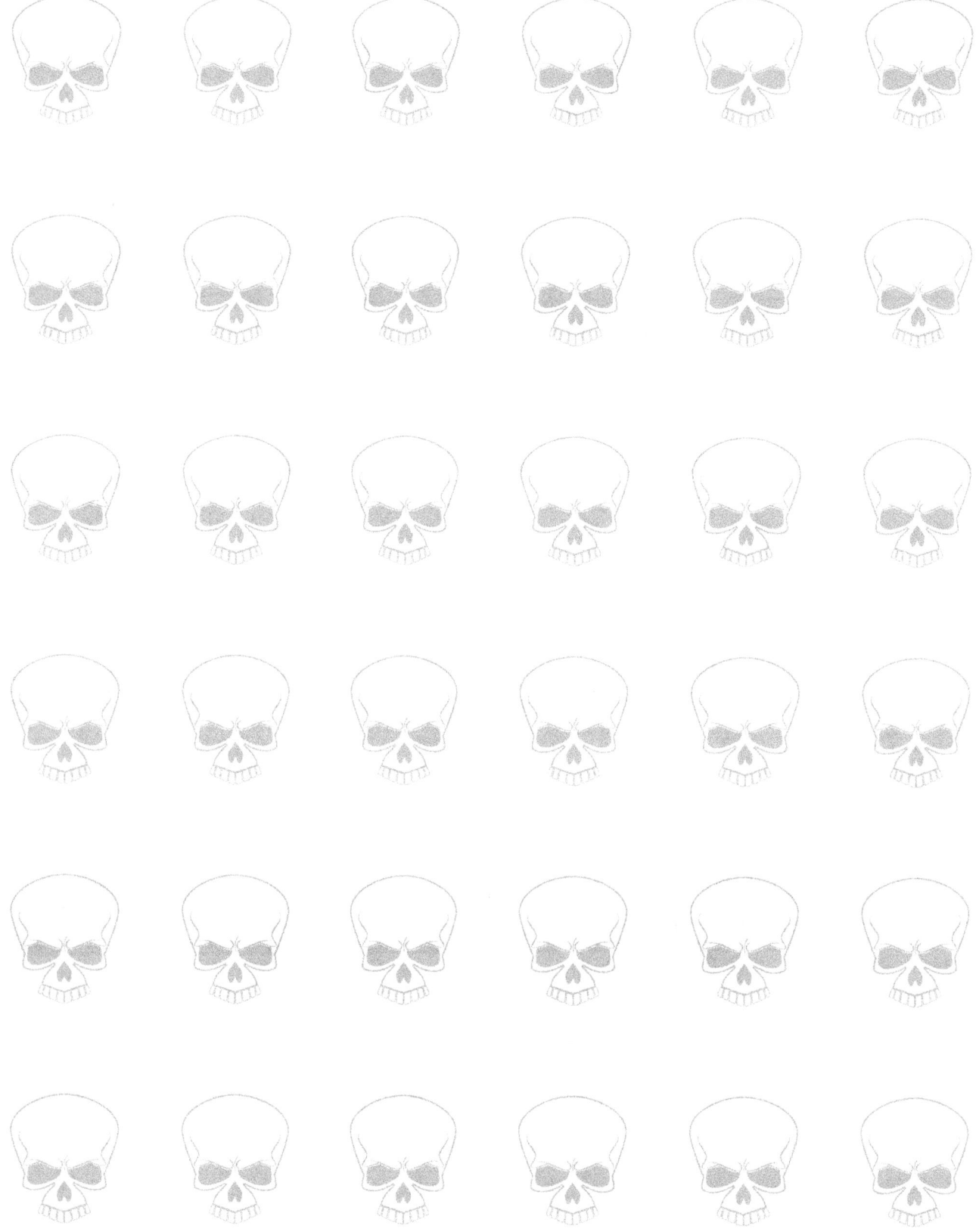

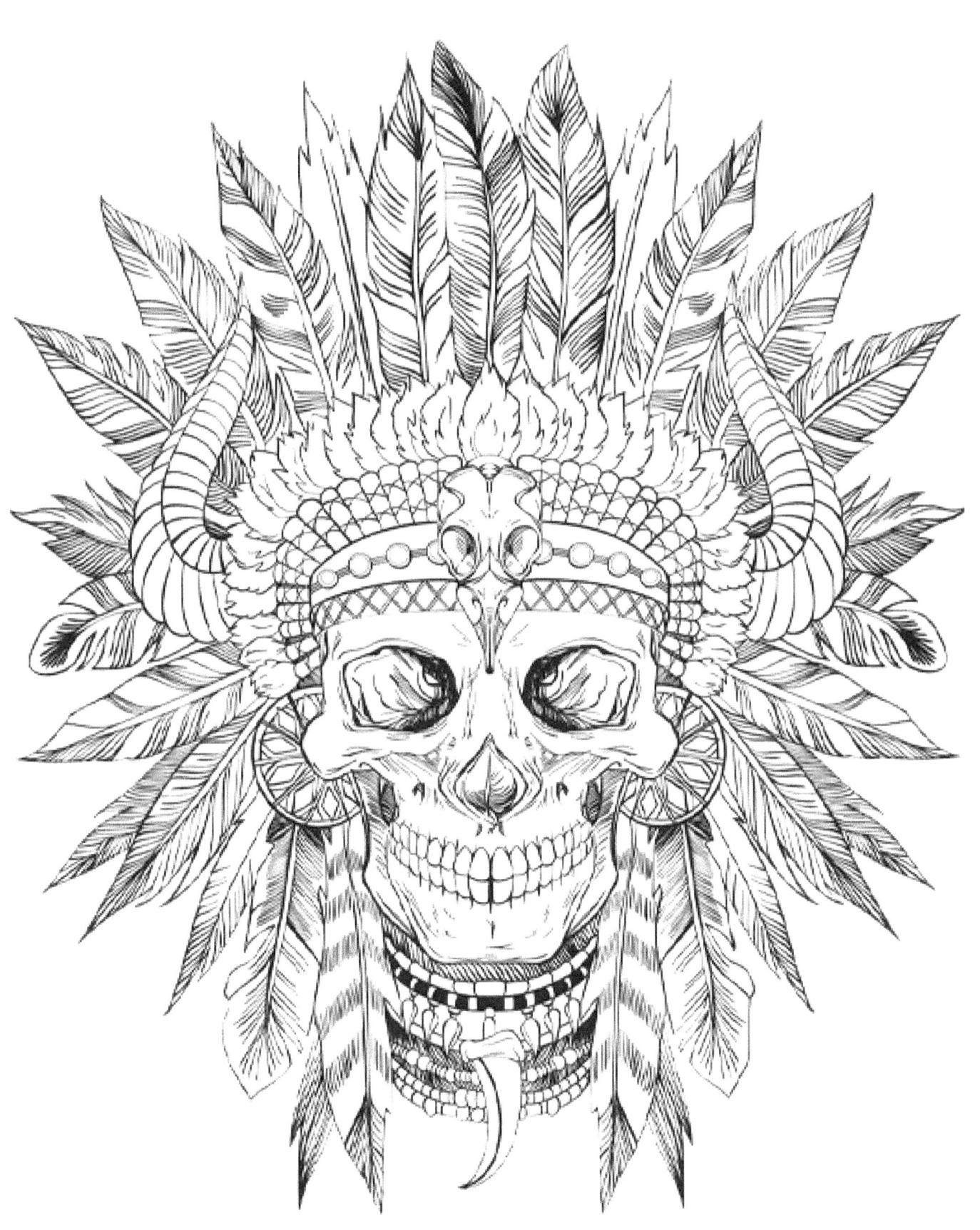

Coloring Test Pages

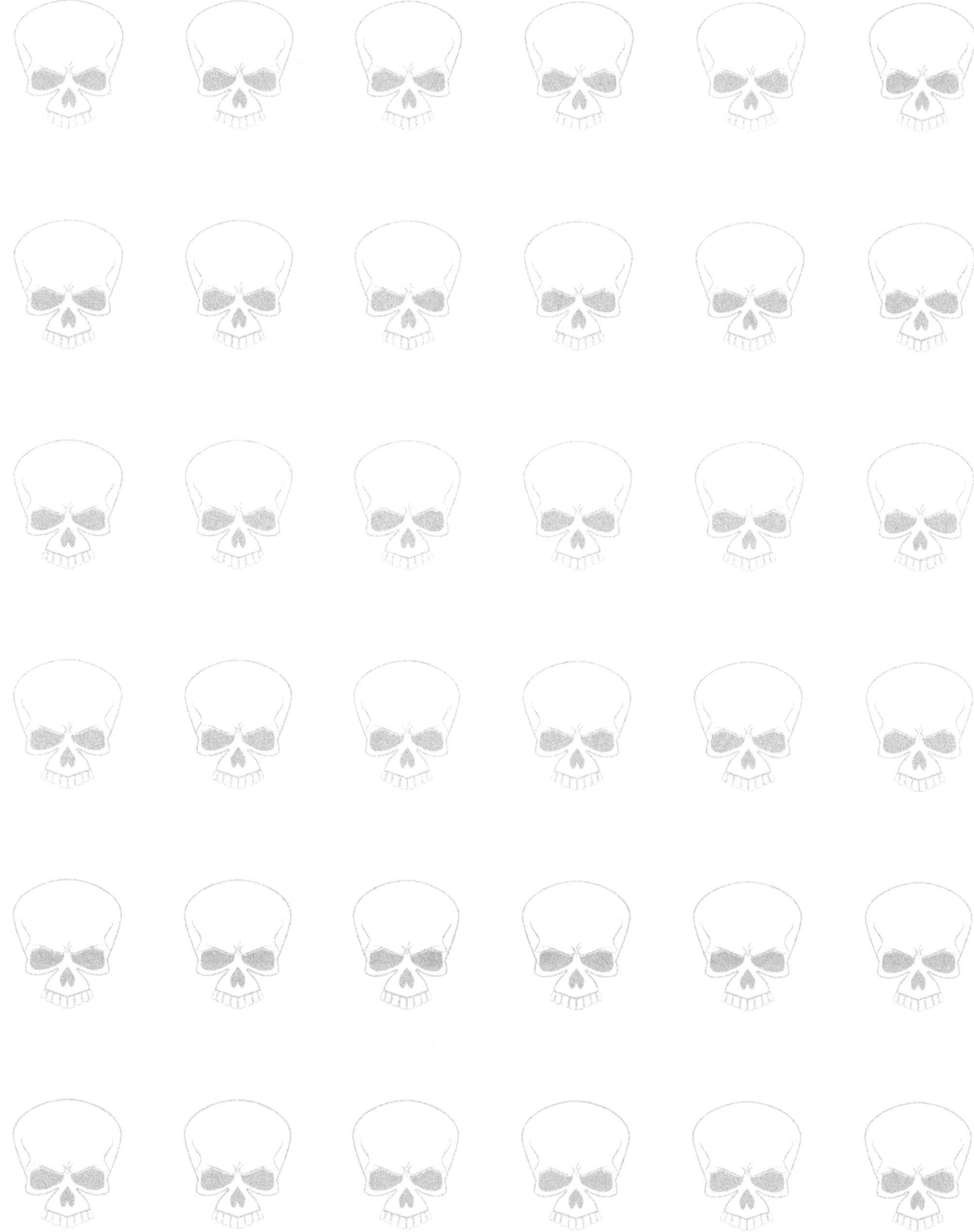

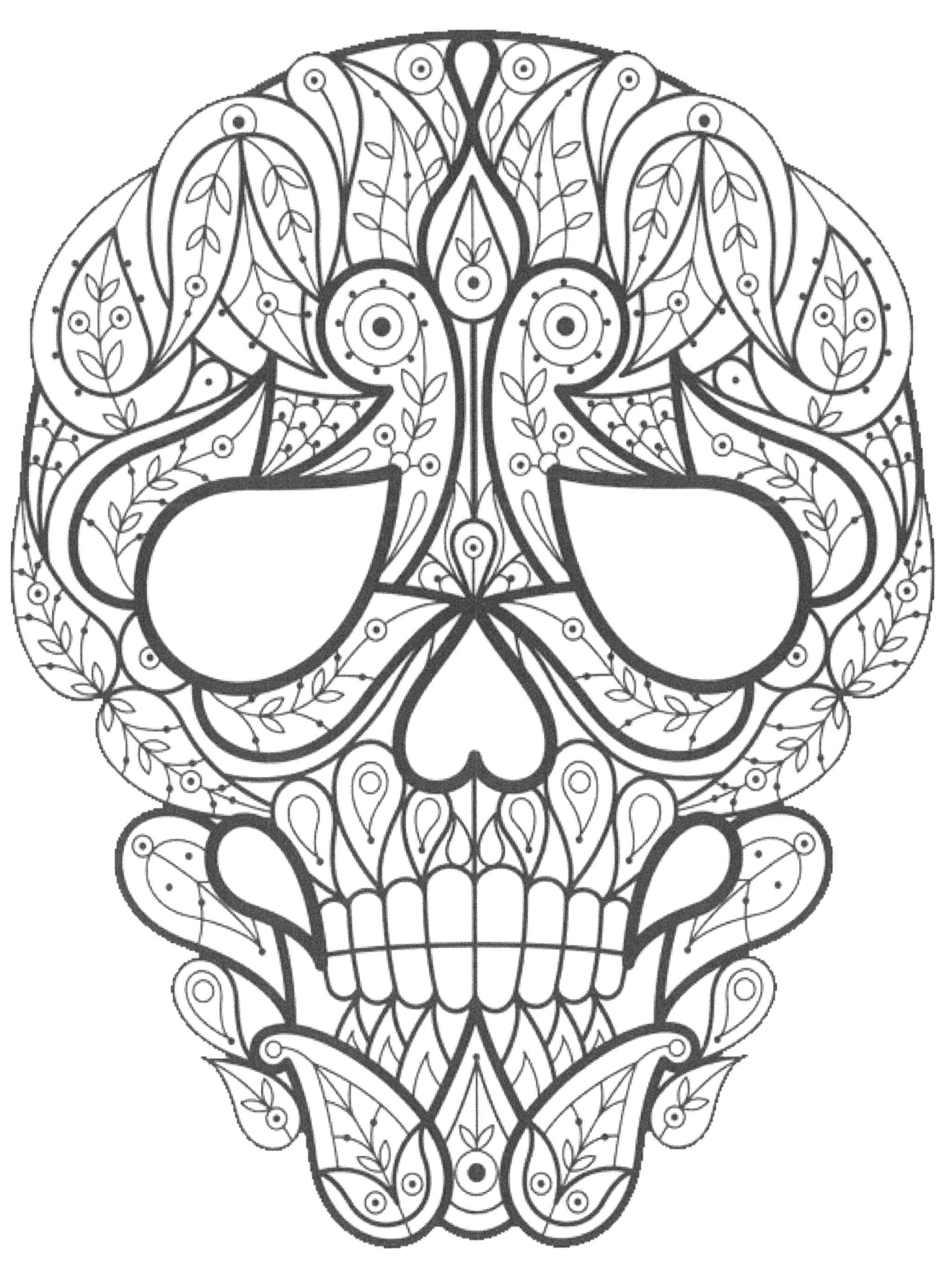